PENGUIN PLAYS

THREE EUROPEAN PLAYS

JEAN ANOUILH was born in Bordeaux in 1910. He studied law at the University of Paris and had his first play, *L'Ermine*, produced in 1932. Since then some thirty of his plays have been performed, of which the best known in England are *Time Remembered*, *Antigone*, *The Lark*, *The Fighting Cock*, *Becket*, *Ring Round the Moon*, *The Waltz of the Toreadors*, *The Cavern* and *Poor Bitos*.

UGO BETTI, a lawyer by profession, was born in 1892. His first play, *La Padrona*, won a prize in 1927, but nearly all his most important plays were written in the five years before his death in 1953. These are *Crime on Goat Island* (1950), *The Joker* (1951), *The Queen and the Rebels* (1951) and *The Burnt Flowerbed* (1953). When Ugo Betti was recognized outside Italy, which was only after his death, three of his plays were running simultaneously in the West End in 1955.

JEAN-PAUL SARTRE was born in Paris in 1905. He taught in Paris for some years before 1946, since when he has spent his time writing, and editing the magazine *Les Temps modernes*. He is a novelist and the founder of French Existentialism as well as a playwright. His plays include *The Flies*, *The Respectable Prostitute*, *Men without Shadows*, *Lucifer and the Lord*, *The Trojan Women*, *Kean*, *Nekrassov* and *Altona*. *Words*, a volume of autobiography, and four of his novels are published in Penguins.

D1202949

THREE EUROPEAN PLAYS

Introduced and Edited by
E. MARTIN BROWNE

RING ROUND THE MOON
Jean Anouilh

THE QUEEN AND THE REBELS
Ugo Betti

IN CAMERA
Jean-Paul Sartre

PENGUIN BOOKS

Penguin Books Ltd, Harmondsworth, Middlesex, England
Penguin Books, 625 Madison Avenue, New York, New York 10022, U.S.A.
Penguin Books Australia Ltd, Ringwood, Victoria, Australia
Penguin Books Canada Ltd, 2801 John Street, Markham, Ontario, Canada L3R 1B4
Penguin Books (N.Z.) Ltd, 182–190 Wairau Road, Auckland 10, New Zealand

—

Ring Round the Moon
First published 1948
This translation published by Methuen 1950
Copyright © Jean Anouilh and Christopher Fry, 1950

The Queen and the Rebels
First published 1949
This translation published by Gollancz 1956
Copyright © Ugo Betti, 1956

In Camera
First published 1944
This translation published by Hamish Hamilton 1946

This selection published in Penguin Books 1958
Reprinted 1960, 1965, 1967, 1969, 1971, 1979

—

Made and printed in Great Britain
by Cox & Wyman Ltd,
London, Reading and Fakenham
Set in Monotype Bembo

CONTENTS

INTRODUCTION

THIS volume contains the first instalment of what we confidently hope to make a large collection from the drama of continental Europe. For while England has been somewhat short of playwrights in the last decade other European countries have been more prolific, France in particular.

In France, the theatre pays more attention to the author than in England; and he does in fact succeed in exercising a considerable influence on the climate of thought instead of merely satisfying the desire for entertainment. He has the advantage of having, on the whole, theatres of smaller size, so that what he has to say can be heard without effort by his audience; and the greater advantage of a public which has always regarded the theatre as a place in which something of note may be said. This is not to say that the public sets any less store by being entertained, but rather that it can be entertained by things of rather more moment than would have a similar result across the Channel.

In this volume are two plays from France which won great success there, but success of a widely different kind. One is of steel, the other of gossamer. But there is a steel structure beneath the gossamer of *Ring Round the Moon*, and a froth of laughter (harsh, perhaps, with fear) rising from the prison-setting in *In Camera*. Between their authors there are many differences, but also, to the eyes of those who see them from a distance as we do, a deeper kind of unity.

The French drama has had a continuous history, with no Cromwell to interrupt it; and it has its roots in two traditions from which it has drawn continuous nourishment even when it has rebelled most hotly against one at least of them.

Classical story and legend have repeated themselves again and again throughout the centuries in French dramatic writing, from the time of Racine to our own day. In the England of the first Elizabeth they may have been as potent an influence as in the France of that time; but the Puritan domination altered the angle from which they were regarded, so that the naturalness with which Portia, at the climax of her fate, compares Bassanio and herself to Hercules and Hesione, would have been impossible a hundred years later. But in France the Classical heritage has remained central to the nation's culture and provided for the writer of today the most potent material with which to draw from his fellow-countrymen a new vision of universal truth in the light of their own thinking.

A good example of this is the *Antigone* of Anouilh. This play adheres closely to the Greek dramatists' version of the legend of the girl who was immured because she insisted on burying her brother's body against the king's orders; but its effect is as different from Sophocles' as is Racine's *Phèdre* from Euripides' *Hippolytus*. The ancient legend has for the modern writer the meaning of his own time: the story is a deathless symbol, and the earth in which he plants his twentieth-century tree has beneath it all the strata of the centuries past, into which the roots of his sapling work their way for nourishment. To Anouilh, writing at the time of the German Occupation, Antigone is the girl who is 'here to say no'. And in fact, despite the skilful cogency of the arguments given to the tyrant Creon which made the play acceptable to the conquerors, the French people saw in his Antigone the expression of their own resistance.

The Occupation must always be remembered in reading works of our time from the Continent, especially perhaps from France. The deep pessimism which informs both the French authors in this volume and most others, arises not only from disturbances in the national spirit which were evident before the war, but even more from that period when the nation found itself deceived by its own leaders and subjected not only to privations and executions but, far more destructively, to the complete loss of certainty or confidence in itself. This is something that the English can hardly understand, for the experience has never been ours: but it is worth the effort of imagination needed to approach it as we read the finest body of drama produced by any single nation since the Second World War.

The other influence which has underlain French drama has been the Catholic. It can scarcely be perceived in the two plays we have here, except that *In Camera* is about hell; the world of these two dramatists seems to take as little account of religion as that of Coward or Rattigan. Christian values cannot be perceived: and in matters of sex Anouilh in particular seems to be totally unaware that they exist at all. Yet it is said that one of the two influences which shaped the youthful thinking of Anouilh was that of Paul Claudel, the fervent Catholic who was at once an Ambassador for France and one of her foremost writers. This is indeed possible, for to Claudel his faith is not a consolation but a demand that no man can fully meet: it does not issue in charity or in progress, nor breed characters of a more humane mould. Rather is it the power which alone can face the inevitable whether in human character or in human destiny. Anouilh has not gained that power, but he has Claudel's clear sight of the human condition.

But to trace an influence upon a single writer is to cloud the vision of what the Catholic faith means in French thought. It is better, perhaps, to remind ourselves that this is one of the basic influences which we may perceive in many forms as we become familiar with French writing. This influence may be seen operating far more directly in the third of our plays, the Italian contribution to this volume.

Ugo Betti was an intensely religious writer. He may be said to deal even more profoundly than Claudel with the Christian view of life, for in his writing it appears in both its religious and its moral aspects. This is natural, for Betti was a lawyer, who became a judge. As a writer, he spent his whole life on the theatre, his first play being dated 1926 (when he was thirty-four years of age) and his last shortly before his death in 1953. Most of his plays are serious, often tragic; a few comedies, of which one (*Summertime*) has been produced in London, were written in the 1930s. From the onset of the War till his death he wrote thirteen plays which many Italians regard as proving him a finer dramatist than Pirandello, the genius of the previous generation. England has yet to know most of these, and it may take English theatregoers time to accustom themselves to a type of setting unlike those they are wont to meet in their native drama. Betti tends towards the bizarre; and clearly prefers to liberate himself from place in the geographical sense–his plays are set in an atmosphere of the mind expressed by a place unlocalized except in so far as the play's story demands it. The present play, with its mysterious room on a frontier showing only the characteristics of troubled times, is a good example though less extreme than most.

The theme which is heard throughout Betti's work is expressed by his brilliant translator, Henry Reed, as 'man's fatal disregard of God'. It is the Catholic doctrine of Original Sin exhibited in terms of contemporary living. *The Queen and the Rebels* is one of his finest works and distils his thought into the experience of a woman who in many ways typifies the human struggle of this time and the response that can be made to its challenge. Argia calls herself 'one of those very common plants that you naturally find growing out of the manure heap of three wars'. She comes into the play 'to go to bed with a man'; she is a slut. But when challenged to play the part of the Queen, she can do it so that she convinces not only the revolutionaries but us that she has a royal spirit. 'For the first time free ... to make decisions that men pause to hear', she faces her enemies and her death:

I believe that God has intentionally made us, not docile, for that He would find useless—but different from Himself and a little too proud—so that we may stand against Him, thwart Him, amaze Him.

Betti may be described as a dramatist in the classic manner: his plays are technically among the best of our century, and made on solid traditional lines. The other two playwrights in this volume are more free and varied in their use of the stage. Of the two, Anouilh has the better sense of theatre: indeed, through a long series of plays no one living has more unfailingly produced the telling theatrical effect at its best.

Jean-Paul Sartre, however, has a unique position in the world of ideas. The philosophy of Existentialism, of which he is the chief public exponent, has made his name famous without being understood as a philosophy; it seems to be better described as an attitude towards man. For Sartre's plays are all concerned with one thing: the freeing of the human spirit. This freedom is gained at the expense of moral values: and the systematic values of Catholicism are of all the most hateful to Sartre. He tried to attack them at length in his longest play *Le Diable et le bon Dieu*. He shows in *Les Mains sales* (translated as *Crime Passionel*) and in *Les Mouches* (*The Flies*) men who are triumphantly themselves by means of murder. He is at pains to omit God from the Universe in which he and his followers believe that no such being exists.

Yet the scene of *Huis clos* is set in hell. Sartre's definition of hell, however, is one which does not postulate any religious conception: the word is, as Mr Harold Hobson puts it in his admirable book, *The French Theatre of Today*, 'a synonym for the ultimate condition of human misery'. Hell in this play is in fact the negation of individual human freedom by means of the permanent incursion of other human beings. . . . 'Hell is other people.' At the dress rehearsal of T. S. Eliot's *The Cocktail Party* the author whispered to me at one moment: 'contre-Sartre'. The line from his play spoken at that moment was 'Hell is oneself.'

Huis clos is Sartre at his most brilliant: it provides a terrifying intellectual experience. Perhaps none of his plays provide more than this: for even here one feels that the characters are in a prison of ideas. It is no accident that the title is a legal phrase: it means 'the period during which the law courts are closed for the vacation'. Neither of the English titles, that of *Vicious Circle* under which the play was produced at the Arts Theatre in 1946, nor the present *In Camera*, do justice to the original concept. One is reminded of Rosalind's answer, in *As You Like It,* to Orlando's question whom Time stays still withal:

With lawyers in the vacation. For they sleep between term and term, and then they perceive not how Time moves.

And timelessly, the prisoners remain confined together in Sartre's hell.

Sartre is famous as a novelist and a philosopher: Jean Anouilh, like Betti, is a writer for the theatre, almost exclusively. As has been said, he is a consummate artist, and *L'Invitation au château* shows him at his most skilful and his most charming. A great success in France, it has won equal success here in the present adaptation by Christopher Fry. Anouilh has much of the poet in his composition, and has been well served indeed by an English dramatic poet who possesses a similar range of linguistic command and poetic fancy. The title *Ring Round the Moon*, more fanciful than the original, is well chosen to convey to the English hearer the quality which he may expect from the play.

Anouilh's considerable output, since his first play *L'Hermine* in 1931, has been classified into *pièces roses* and *pièces noires*. Not all the plays fit easily into either category; but *Ring Round the Moon* comes unquestionably into the former. It even has that rarity, a happy ending; it is as ebullient as the fireworks with which it concludes. Yet even here can be perceived the deep pessimism, and the absence, the apparent unconsciousness, of moral values, which characterize this dramatist's work. In Anouilh's world the heroine is a gentle girl to whom the world does terrible things: she is a pure being, whom the world sullies and often destroys. But her own behaviour seems to us to negate the very idea of purity: and we find ourselves asking what the word, of which Anouilh is very fond, can mean for him. The answer would seem to be that for him the moral values as we know them do not exist: purity is for him the preservation of one's own nature.

Once this is grasped, we are able to enjoy the overflowing gallery of portraits so vividly drawn in his plays, which afford the richest of entertainment. *Ring Round the Moon* is a fine example. Christopher Fry has, wisely no doubt, concealed that element in Isabelle's situation which would make her less than a heroine to English sensibilities; and he has translated deliciously the idiosyncrasies of the author's other creations.

Cross-channel passages have always been risky for plays, but Anouilh has such supreme gifts as a dramatist that even when we find his view of life harsh, his language sometimes unpleasant, his philosophy depressing, we cannot help going back to him for the genius with which he can excite us in a theatre.

E. MARTIN BROWNE

Note: I am indebted in many respects to Mr Harold Hobson's book mentioned above, *The French Theatre of Today* (Harrap), which I recommend to anyone wanting to pursue the subject.

JEAN ANOUILH

Ring Round the Moon

A CHARADE WITH MUSIC

L'Invitation au château

TRANSLATED BY
CHRISTOPHER FRY

RING ROUND THE MOON

This play was first presented at the Globe Theatre, London, by Tennent Productions Ltd (in association with the Arts Council of Great Britain) on 26 January 1950, with the following cast:

JOSHUA, *a crumbling butler*	David Horne
HUGO, *a young man-about-town*	Paul Scofield
FREDERIC, *his brother, in love with*	Paul Scofield
DIANA MESSERSCHMANN, *engaged to Frederic, secretly in love with Hugo*	Audrey Fildes
LADY INDIA, *Messerschmann's mistress, secretly in love with*	Marjorie Stewart
PATRICE BOMBELLES, *Messerschmann's secretive secretary*	Richard Wattis
MADAME DESMERMORTES, *Aunt to Hugo, Frederic, and Lady India*	Margaret Rutherford
CAPULAT, *her faded companion*	Daphne Newton
MESSERSCHMANN, *Diana's father, a melancholy millionaire*	Cecil Trouncer
ROMAINVILLE, *a lepidopterist, patron of*	William Mervyn
ISABELLE, *a ballet dancer*	Claire Bloom
HER MOTHER, *a teacher of the pianoforte*	Mona Washbourne
A GENERAL	Mayne Lynton
FOOTMEN	Richard Scott
	David Phethean

SCENE

The play takes place in a winter-garden, in spring

ACT ONE

SCENE I

*A rococo winter-garden; glass and wrought-iron; yellow plush curtains and
green plants. It looks out on to a wide expanse of park.*

Enter JOSHUA, *a butler, and* HUGO, *a young man-about-town, smoking
a fat cigar.*

HUGO: And how about last night, Joshua? Did the same thing
happen?

JOSHUA: I'm sorry I can't deny it, Mr Hugo, but the same thing
did.

HUGO: My brother slept all night under her window?

JOSHUA: Yes, Mr Hugo – under both her windows. For five nights
now Mr Frederic has gone to bed in a rhododendron bush: you
know, sir, the one on the south side of the west wing, beside
that statue they call Calliope, a classical character, sir. Every morning the housemaid has found his bed unrumpled, and the gardener
has found the rhododendrons rumpled. Well, it gives them a jolt,
Mr Hugo, as who wouldn't it? I try to make light of it, so as to
keep them in the dark: but one day they'll talk and Madam will
know all about it.

HUGO: Have you ever been in love, Joshua?

JOSHUA: Now, sir, think: I've been in service with Madam for
thirty years; I'm too old.

HUGO: But before that?

JOSHUA: I was too young.

HUGO: Mine's the age for it, Joshua. I fall in love as a matter of
routine. But not ludicrously like my brother.

JOSHUA: No, sir. Mr Frederic hasn't your style at all, sir.

HUGO: And yet we're the same age. It's odd, isn't it?

JOSHUA: You're ten minutes older, sir, remember that.

HUGO: Yes, I know. But who would have thought that those ten
minutes would have taught me so much about women?

JOSHUA: The young lady knows she can do what she likes with your brother, sir.

HUGO: She may think she knows. But – I've schemed a scheme.

JOSHUA: I'm glad to hear that, Mr Hugo.

HUGO: I got up early this morning because I've decided to take action. This dawn is the dawn of the unexpected. What's the time?

JOSHUA: Twelve o'clock, Mr Hugo.

HUGO: By twelve-thirty, Joshua, I shall begin to loom big on the horizon.

JOSHUA: Oh, and Mr Hugo, sir – I attempted to explain away the rhododendrons, sir, by informing the gardener that a wolf had been observed making depredations in the vicinity, sir. I told him not to mention this, sir, on the grounds that it might occasion the guests a measure of comprehensible alarm, sir . . . Thank you, sir.

[*Exit* HUGO. *Enter* FREDERIC. *It is the same actor.*]

FREDERIC: Joshua!

JOSHUA: Mr Frederic?

FREDERIC: Has Miss Diana come down yet?

JOSHUA: Not yet, Mr Frederic.

FREDERIC: Do I look tired, Joshua?

JOSHUA: If I may be allowed to be frank, yes, you do, sir.

FREDERIC: But you're quite mistaken, you know. I've never slept better.

JOSHUA: I think I ought to tell you, sir, the gardener's intending to set wolf-traps in the rhododendrons.

FREDERIC: Never mind, Joshua. I'll sleep in the azaleas.

JOSHUA: And the housemaid, sir, the one who looks after the west wing, she has been making remarks of horrified dissatisfaction. She came to see me quite ready to drop.

FREDERIC: Tell her, next time, to drop into my bed, if she would be so good, and untidy it herself.

JOSHUA: Oh, Mr Frederic!

FREDERIC: Why not? She's very charming. And when she's unmade it sufficiently she will be able to make it again, and everything will seem to be just as usual.

JOSHUA: Very good, Mr Frederic.

[*Exit* JOSHUA. *Enter* DIANA.]

FREDERIC: Diana! How good to see you again. It's been like a lifetime since yesterday.

DIANA [*stopping and looking at him*]: Which one of you is it now?

FREDERIC [*reproachfully*]: Oh, Diana; that's not a nice thing to ask me!

DIANA: Ah yes, it is you. You're looking at me like a little lost dog again. Did you get up on the wrong side of the rhododendrons? At first you looked so triumphant I thought you were your brother.

FREDERIC: If you prefer him to me, I shall go away and die.

DIANA: Dear Frederic! You know I should only mistake you by accident. You're so alike.

FREDERIC: Our hearts aren't alike.

DIANA: No, that's true. But imagine me alone in the park one evening: I hear the twigs cracking behind me and what sounds like your step: two arms go round me, and they feel like your arms: a mouth kisses me, and it feels like your mouth. How am I to have time to make sure it's the right heart, Frederic?

FREDERIC: But, Diana, I've never put my arms round you in the park.

DIANA: Are you sure?

FREDERIC: Perfectly sure. Diana! It was my brother, looking like me on purpose! It was my double, double-crossing me again! I must find him: I've got to speak to him!

DIANA [*laughing and stopping him*]: Now, dear, dear, *dear, dear, dear* Frederic! Don't go rushing to conclusions. I made it up. No one's been kissing me.

FREDERIC [*hanging his head*]: I beg your pardon, Diana. I completely believe you. But if Hugo loved you, I should kill myself.

DIANA: That would be terrible. I should never be sure which of you was dead. [*She is pensive a moment.*] Of course it would be a great help to your brother; he would only have to drop a few tears for you at the funeral, and then come and whisper in my ear, 'Ssh: don't tell anyone! They've made a great mistake. This is really Hugo's funeral!' How should I answer that?

FREDERIC: But you couldn't be deceived for a moment, could you? If I were so exactly like Hugo, in word and thought and deed, I should *be* Hugo.

DIANA: Yes, that's true.

FREDERIC [*after a pause*]: Diana, it's Hugo you love! Good-bye.

DIANA: Are you mad? I hate him. Kiss me.

FREDERIC [*lost*]: Diana!

DIANA: Kiss me, you lost dog, and I'll find your way home for you.

FREDERIC: I love you.

DIANA: I love you, too, Frederic.

[*They kiss.*]

I suppose you're quite sure you're not Hugo? He's capable of absolutely anything.

[*They go. Enter* LADY INDIA *and* PATRICE BOMBELLES.]

PATRICE: Anything! Anything! He's capable of absolutely anything!

LADY INDIA: But, dear heart, how could he suspect us? We've been so careful.

PATRICE: I tell you, I wouldn't trust that fellow Hugo an inch. Yesterday he giggled at me. Quite noticeably, as I went past him. Why should he have giggled if he didn't know all about us?

LADY INDIA: When did he giggle?

PATRICE: Last night, on the terrace, after dinner.

LADY INDIA: Last night? We were all there together. He choked himself with cigar smoke. He was coughing.

PATRICE: He was coughing to disguise his giggle, but that didn't deceive me for a moment.

LADY INDIA: Anyway, why should this young man, who has nothing to do with me, giggle because he's found out we're having an affair?

PATRICE: Never mind why; mistrust him. To begin with there's this fantastic likeness to his brother.

LADY INDIA: He can't help that.

PATRICE: My dear Dorothy! If he had any sense of propriety, he would never allow it to go on. He revels in it; he copies his brother's clothes.

LADY INDIA: No, dear, Frederic copies his.

PATRICE: Well, it's the same thing. Now, I have eight brothers –

LADY INDIA: And they all look exactly like you?

PATRICE: Not at all.

LADY INDIA: I see; then it doesn't help to convince me that this boy would say anything to Messerschmann.

PATRICE: *Say* anything, no; but little jokes and innuendoes when we're all in the drawing-room, yes; a mysterious chuckle in the middle of a meal, or a giggle like the one you thought was choking him with cigar-smoke; yes, most certainly.

LADY INDIA: Little jokes and chuckles will pass right over Messerschmann's head. He suffers from terribly poor reception.

PATRICE: It's we who would have a poor reception if once he knew. Don't forget, you're his mistress and I'm his private secretary. We're both completely dependent on your magnate.

LADY INDIA [reproachfully]: Dearest heart, you use the most curious words.

PATRICE: Magnate?

LADY INDIA: No.

PATRICE: Private secretary?

LADY INDIA: No. [She leans against him.] Patrice, darling, I know I give him the pleasure of paying my bills, and every night I let him trail along to my room to kiss my hand; but that means nothing, and you mean everything.

PATRICE [desperately]: Dorothy! We're in the winter-garden –

LADY INDIA: On a lovely spring morning.

PATRICE: The season is immaterial! All this glass! Everyone can see us! We're completely exposed.

LADY INDIA: Danger! Oh, that's wonderful; I love it; I like being mad more than anything. Did I ever tell you about the evening in Monte Carlo when I went to a little dockside café, absolutely naked except for a cloak and my diamonds? Quite alone, too, amongst all those drunken brutes.

PATRICE: At Monte Carlo?

LADY INDIA: A little café where the croupiers used to sip a secret Bock between sessions. I just smiled to see how their hands shook when they raised their glasses . . . So let him come, let him catch us, let him murder us! I shall drive him off with a lash of contempt! . . . It will be magnificent!

PATRICE: Yes.

LADY INDIA: Don't forget you belong to a most distinguished family, Patrice, and I, after all, am Lady India. He should be very grateful that we take the trouble to infuriate him. Money isn't everything.

[They go.]

[Enter MME DESMERMORTES, in a wheel-chair, pushed by her companion, CAPULAT, and HUGO.]

MME DESMER: Money is nothing! Oodles, oodles, oodles? Whatever do you mean, Hugo, that Mr Messerschmann has oodles?

HUGO: He's as rich as Croesus.

MME DESMER: Oh, I see – but whatever does he do with it all?

HUGO: Eats noodles.

MME DESMER: You're being absolutely too playful, Hugo.

HUGO: It's quite true. At every meal, without butter or salt, and drinks water.

MME DESMER: How very spectacular. And you tell me that Dorothy India is ruining him?

HUGO: She would be, if anyone could be, but there's too much of it even for her.

MME DESMER [remembering CAPULAT]: You're a scandal-monger, Hugo. You forget I'm your aunt, and India's aunt. I won't listen to you. I'm an elderly woman, and I never listen to anyone. Capulat, go and look for my handkerchief.

[CAPULAT goes.]

Now, between ourselves, do you really imagine he's keeping her?

HUGO: Between ourselves, without a shadow of doubt.

MME DESMER: It's monstrous, Hugo; humiliating.

HUGO: Utterly monstrous, but, between ourselves, why humiliating?

MME DESMER: She is a FitzHenry! And through me, a Desmermortes. If only your uncle Antony were alive it would kill him. Hugo, people are so unkind; they will think I invited Dorothy and this nabob at the same time on purpose. They'll say I'm a party to it. So should I.

HUGO: Everyone knows you invited Mr Messerschmann and his daughter because Frederic asked you to. Frederic is going to announce his engagement to Diana tomorrow.

MME DESMER: Yes. There's another puppy-witted piece of folly! Fancy becoming so infatuated with that girl he even has to ask her to marry him! When he was little he always looked so sad and resigned when he came to kiss me on Christmas morning. I used to call him St Pancras. And now the poor lamb's to be sacrificed. Can you bear to think of him being delivered over, gagged and bound, in his morning coat and gardenia, to this Diana Messerschmann and her millions?

HUGO: No, Aunt.

MME DESMER: No, I should think not. If it had been you, it would have been different. I love it when the lamb turns round and eats up the high priest. But with poor little Frederic it won't even be funny.

HUGO: If the marriage takes place, Aunt.

MME DESMER [*with a sigh*]: And who can prevent it now?

HUGO: Who knows who?

[CAPULAT *returns.*]

CAPULAT: Here is your handkerchief, madam.

MME DESMER: Thank you, my dear. Trundle me into the sun, if you will.

[*Enter* MESSERSCHMANN *and* ROMAINVILLE.]

Good morning, dear Romainville! Good morning, Mr Messerschmann. Have you had a good night's rest?

MESSER: I never sleep, madam.

MME DESMER: Neither do I. We must make an appointment with one another some time, and gossip while the rest of them snore. We can say the most terrible things about them; it will help to kill time. He takes such a lot of killing, that animal, don't you think? I'm a wicked person, Mr Messerschmann. Are you?

MESSER: I told you so, madam.

MME DESMER: How nice. We can be wicked together. That will amuse me very much. Push, dear, trundle me away. I told you I wanted to be in the sun. Oh, Mr Messerschmann, my butler tells me you only eat noodles?

MESSER: That is so, without butter and without salt.

MME DESMER: And I believe you're a great friend of my niece, Dorothy?

MESSER: Yes, I have the pleasure of Lady India's friendship.

MME DESMER: Insomnia, Dorothy, and nothing but noodles! What a *very* interesting life . . .

[*They go.* ROMAINVILLE *tries to escape to avoid* HUGO.]

HUGO [*catching him*]: Her train gets in at twelve-thirty.

ROMAINVILLE: No!

HUGO: It certainly does.

ROMAINVILLE: I'm convinced it's all a great mistake. It's making me ill with nerves. Are you sure you're not mad?

HUGO: Quite sure. How about you?

ROMAINVILLE: Not at all sure. Suppose I don't cooperate?

HUGO: A scandal, Romainville.

ROMAINVILLE [*losing his temper*]: What scandal, for God's sake? My relationship with this girl is absolutely irreproachable.

HUGO: Suppose I say to my aunt, 'Our dear Romainville, feeling the approach of springtime in the air, and in order to make his visit to you a cheerful one, has fetched his little friend over to stay at the inn at St Fleur: he goes to see her secretly three times a week.' What do you say then?

ROMAINVILLE: That it isn't true! That I'm only interested in this girl as I'm interested in butterflies and old furniture. Is it my fault if I'm known as a patron of the arts?

HUGO: No.

ROMAINVILLE: The child needed a holiday before she goes back into the ballet. She was rather pale – do understand that, Hugo – she was extremely pale. Anybody would have done the same thing. It's entirely a question of common humanity. I said to her: Come and spend a few days at Auvergne with your mother. Who, for God's sake, is going to make trouble because I give a holiday to a poor girl who needs one? Certainly not your good aunt, who buttonholes me every year for her local charities.

HUGO: To a poor girl who needs a holiday, no. But to your mistress, Romainville – well, you know my aunt.

ROMAINVILLE: For God's sake, she isn't my mistress! I assure you she isn't, not the least bit.

HUGO: Who's going to believe you?

ROMAINVILLE: Everybody – because it's true.

HUGO: That's no help. It doesn't seem likely.

ROMAINVILLE: So according to you the truth means nothing.

HUGO: Nothing, dear boy, if no one believes it.

[*The sound of a dinner gong.*]

Let's go amiably in to lunch. They'll be here any minute now. I've warned Joshua and he'll let me know. I shall come out and have a word with them, and then, during coffee, Joshua can tell my aunt that your niece has arrived.

ROMAINVILLE: But suppose my real niece comes on the same train?

HUGO: That's all right. I sent her a telegram from you; you told her that my aunt's invitation had been cancelled for the time being.

ROMAINVILLE: It's a trap! And all because you found me drinking an innocent orangeade with this little girl, in a cake-shop at St Fleur!

HUGO: Exactly.

ROMAINVILLE: You're the devil!

HUGO: Almost.

ROMAINVILLE: Would you just tell me what you're up to?

HUGO: A huge and dark design.

[*The gong sounds again.*]

There's the second gong. So in to luncheon, Romainville. You shall know everything before you're much older.

[*They go.*

The stage is empty for a moment, then JOSHUA *shows in* ISABELLE *and her* MOTHER *with their suitcases.*]

JOSHUA: If the ladies would be so good as to take a seat, I will go and inform Mr Hugo of their arrival.

[*He goes.*]

THE MOTHER: Isn't it luxurious, Isabelle? Such taste! Such grandeur! Now this is the kind of atmosphere where I really feel myself.

ISABELLE: Yes, Mother.

THE MOTHER: Some people, you know, can only breathe where there's beauty and luxury. Take luxury away from them and they go quite limp.

ISABELLE: Yes, Mother.

THE MOTHER: Always remember, Isabelle, your grandfather was the biggest wallpaper dealer in the town. We've even had two servants at the same time, not counting the shop-assistants, of course. When I was your age your grandmother would never have let me go out alone.

ISABELLE: No, Mother.

THE MOTHER: No. The maid always followed three steps behind me. Three steps. It was wonderful.

ISABELLE: Yes, Mother.

THE MOTHER: Did you see the butler?

ISABELLE: Yes, Mother.

THE MOTHER: That dignity, that sort of quilted voice, extremely polite but also slightly scornful, such a perfect manner. [*She mimics him, delightedly.*] 'If the ladies would be so good as to take a seat.'

'To take a seat!' You see how beautifully he chose his words! . . . You know, dear, in my dreams of you, there's always a butler like that in the background.

ISABELLE: Oh, Mother, you know it's not –

THE MOTHER: Ah yes, there is. It's been a dream of mine that you shall have everything I've missed. I don't say much, I know, but there are times when I suffer. For instance, when I see your hands getting rough and red from washing-up . . .

ISABELLE: Now, please, Mother –

THE MOTHER: I know it means nothing to you, because you haven't my sensitive nature. And I know I don't help you as much as I should. If only I were a little stronger; but even so I have to think of my art, I have to preserve my hands for my piano. And then I never knew what it was to want for anything when I was a girl, so different from you, my poor child, so I mustn't expect you to understand me. You roll up your sleeves, you sing something, and abracadabra everything's done; you think no more about it.

ISABELLE: It's the best way, Mother.

THE MOTHER: I admire you for it. But with my upbringing, and all my dreams which came to nothing, I could never do it. I still have dreams, but now they're for you, Isabelle: a quite different future for you, a future of luxury and beauty, with a little corner somewhere for your mother. You're artistic, you're pretty, a little more commonplace than I was, perhaps – that's owing to your father – but interesting and attractive. You will certainly please someone, I'm sure you will. What do you suppose the young man wants you here for?

[Enter HUGO.]

HUGO: Thank you for being so punctual.

THE MOTHER: Not at all. Punctuality is the politeness of princes, I always think. And I'm sure you'll agree with me.

HUGO: Oh yes, indeed. And this is Miss Isabelle? . . . I wasn't mistaken.

THE MOTHER: She's a charming child.

HUGO: More than charming.

THE MOTHER: Mr Romainville must have spoken about her to you.

HUGO [not taking his eyes from ISABELLE]: He has indeed.

THE MOTHER: He is one of our dear Parisian friends.

HUGO [*rather coldly*]: Yes, I know. How do you feel about this adventure, Miss Isabelle? The most essential thing is for you to enjoy it.

THE MOTHER: She is thrilled about it!

ISABELLE: All Mr Romainville said was that you had asked us up to your house this evening.

HUGO: Nothing else?

ISABELLE: No, nothing.

THE MOTHER: I expect our friend meant it all to be a surprise.

HUGO: And why should you think I would ask you to come here?

ISABELLE: I don't know. To dance, I expect. I am a dancer.

HUGO: Not only to dance.

THE MOTHER: Not only to dance? Now you're beginning to make me really inquisitive.

HUGO: There's a ball being held in this house tonight. I need you here to be very beautiful, more beautiful, indeed, than anyone else.

ISABELLE: I?

HUGO: Yes. Are you afraid?

ISABELLE: A little. I'm not very beautiful, and so I wonder –

HUGO: I rang up Paris this morning. Roeseda Soeurs are sending some dresses to choose from, and their best fitters. At the first note of the violins, you will be ready.

ISABELLE: But what am I supposed to do?

HUGO: Only to go serenely through the night like a butterfly venturing on moonlight. With the first light of day we'll set you free. [*To the* MOTHER]: The engagement will be paid for in the usual way, and the dress will be hers.

THE MOTHER [*simpering*]: Oh, but we didn't think for one moment –

HUGO: But I thought. Now I must go back to the dining-room or they'll begin to wonder where I am. I'm sorry I can't make it less of a mystery for you. Here is Joshua to show you to your rooms. He will bring you your lunch. No one must know you're in the house. As soon as I can I shall come and tell you what I want you to do.

[*He goes.* JOSHUA *takes the suitcases.*]

JOSHUA: If the ladies will be so good as to follow me.

THE MOTHER: Thank you very much. What a distinguished boy,

such beautiful manners. Did you not notice, dear, how he kissed my hand? Wake up, dear, are you dreaming?

ISABELLE: No, Mother. Is he the one they call Hugo? Is he the one who asked us here?

THE MOTHER: Well, of course. So handsome, don't you think? Now come along, we're keeping the butler waiting. Where are you, my dear, in the moon?

ISABELLE [*in a strange voice, following*]: Yes, Mother.

CURTAIN

SCENE 2

The same scene. The same evening.
MADAME DESMERMORTES *alone.*

MME DESMER: Capulat! Capulat! What on earth can she be up to? Capulat! Really, how marooned one is away from a bell-rope. I might be Robinson Crusoe, and without any of his initiative. If only one's governess, when one was a girl, had taught one something practical like running up a flag of distress or firing a gun.

[JOSHUA *enters.*]

Thank heaven I'm on some sort of navigation route! Joshua! Joshua!... Ah, Cap Griz-Nez! Joshua! Put into land for a moment, my dear man, and rescue me. I was washed up here fifteen minutes ago, and I haven't seen a living creature since.

JOSHUA: Not one, madam?

MME DESMER: Not one, and they say the world is overpopulated. I sent Mlle Capulat to fetch the list of guests out of my bureau. You would think I'd ask her to restock the lake with carp, the time it's taking her.

[CAPULAT *enters.*]

Oh, there you are at last, Capulat. You left me here with a broken brake, and I've had nothing to do but to think over all my short-comings, *twice*. If you'd been away any longer I should have started to regret them. Where have you been?

CAPULAT: You said the list was in the left-hand bottom drawer, madam, but it was the right-hand top drawer.

MME DESMER: That's just another way of looking at it. [*She takes the list from* CAPULAT.] Now . . . well, get to work . . . I must try and remember who all these names belong to. It is so difficult. Nowadays no one has any proper sense of family; people have perfectly good names and then go and produce the most unpredictable faces to go with them. I don't know how they expect to be recognized; and, worse still, it encourages all those terrible people who go to parties without being asked. I remember an evening at the Baroness Grave-Toureau's . . . where is everybody? Capulat, are you listening? . . . I was saying, I remember an evening at the Baroness Grave-Toureau's when . . . well, mend me – mend me! . . . Joshua, I remember an evening at the Baroness Grave-Toureau's when there were so many uninvited guests the Baroness imagined she must be at someone else's party, and spent most of the evening looking for her hostess to say good-bye. Now . . . must you do that? Oh! Deliverance! . . . Now, Joshua, did you hear what I was saying to Capulat? We don't want an unfortunate episode like that. Do you understand, Joshua, we don't want any mistakes.

JOSHUA: Certainly not, madam; though as madam says, faces these days have taken a haphazard turn, most inconsiderate.

MME DESMER: You will have to look into them very carefully, Joshua, and so shall I. If one stares fixedly at an interloper's frontal bone, fixedly, Joshua, for a count of nine, a look of guilt will steal over it at once. Remember that, Joshua. I intend to stare myself, with great penetration, whenever the occasion offers.

JOSHUA: I hope and trust, madam, that no such occasional offering will ensue. It would be a cloud on an evening of otherwise nice and aristocratic joy, which none of us would like to have to denounce, madam.

MME DESMER: You're crumbling into a benevolent old man, Joshua. Denouncing – that's delicious; and I depend on you to see that we have no trespassers. Come with me now, and we'll make a last inspection of the battlefield. Well, Capulat, well, my dear.

CAPULAT: I feel so excited, madam, like a little yeasty bun in a good oven, really I do.

MME DESMER: How splendid! And no doubt the buns feel like little

Capulats . . . Now, the Prince of Palenge, what on earth does he look like, Joshua? Oh, yes, yes, I remember; like a rather half-hearted resolution with a Balaclava beard . . .

[*The chair starts suddenly and* MADAME DESMERMORTES *rolls out followed by* CAPULAT *and* JOSHUA. *After a moment,* HUGO *and* ISABELLE *enter.*]

HUGO: All right; now just walk a few steps towards me. Turn. Walk away again. You're perfect. What on earth are you trembling for?

ISABELLE: Scared.

HUGO: Scared of what? Of going to a party?

ISABELLE: Yes, I suppose so. The violins tuning up, a house full of strange people all at this moment dressing for the great occasion; and scared of the mystery you're making of it.

HUGO: And scared of me?

ISABELLE: Very much.

HUGO: You think I'm going to drag you into some shameful scene or other. Romainville has been maligning me.

ISABELLE: He said –

HUGO: And of course you believed him?

ISABELLE [*gently*]: No.

HUGO: You should have believed him. When you discover what I've planned for this evening, you'll think I'm even worse than Romain-ville imagines. But you don't have to be afraid of bad people; they're just poor complicated devils like everyone else. It's only the fools who are formidable.

[*Enter* ROMAINVILLE.]

And here he is. We were talking about you. How are you this evening?

ROMAINVILLE: Very poorly, very poorly indeed. I'd been looking forward to this party very much, but I feel now as though I were going to an execution. I can't see why you want to go on with it.

HUGO: He's afraid you'll lose your head among the knives and forks, or use a dessert-spoon on the foie-gras, and they'll leap to their feet and say, 'This can't be his niece at all! She's an impostor!' . . . Just walk away a little; now turn. Look at that, Romainville. There's a niece for you! Between ourselves, old man, what's your niece really like?

ROMAINVILLE [*stiffly*]: She's a rather plain girl. Her nose is perhaps not as small as others. But she has an extremely nice character.

HUGO: It's clearly high time you replaced her. Look at this girl in a dress like the smoke of bonfires. You'll never see a niece more transparent, less of this world, or so entirely fashioned for a singular night of dancing in the early summer.

ROMAINVILLE [*solemnly inspecting her*]: Hold yourself upright. When you're presented to people don't address them by their titles. Always wait for an old person to speak to you.

HUGO: Dear me, you're wasting your breath. Isabelle was waiting for older people to speak to her in the womb. My aunt has an infallible instinct for quality, and she's given her a room looking out on to the garden. If she hadn't had the highest opinion of her, she would have put her facing the park.

ROMAINVILLE: Not at all; I'm facing the park.

HUGO [*laughing*]: So you see what I mean!

[THE MOTHER *enters.*]

THE MOTHER: May I come in? May I come in? I couldn't keep away for another minute; I simply had to come and see the dress.

HUGO [*going to her, vexed*]: I thought it was agreed you should stay in your room. We don't want people asking who you are.

THE MOTHER: I came on tiptoe the whole way; you would have thought I was a shadow. I'm dying of curiosity. Oh, how charming! Oh, how wonderfully elegant! Hold yourself up straight, dear. What good taste! I'm quite sure Mr Hugo chose it himself.

HUGO: Not at all. Your daughter chose it.

THE MOTHER: Then I'm sure you had something to do with it. Or else the child guessed your taste and chose it to please you.

ISABELLE: Mother!

THE MOTHER: Turn round, dear. Once again. Hold yourself up. She's a constant surprise to me. Dressed, you would think she's *such* a skinnygalee; undressed, she's almost plump. Raspoutini her ballet-master said it's quite simply because she is well built. As a matter of fact, and I don't say it just because I'm her mother, she has very good legs. This dear gentleman can bear me out, can't you?

ROMAINVILLE [*embarrassed*]: Hm! I still think she looks extremely pale. We should give her a tonic. That's it, a splendid tonic.

THE MOTHER: Pale! How can you say so? Look at her, she's as pink as a strawberry.

ROMAINVILLE: Hm! The country-air has done some good already, you see. There's nothing like the country, nothing like it.

THE MOTHER: How can you say so? The country is death to her. And to me. We're just hothouse flowers, two Parisians, two artists. In the countryside we just wait to be eaten by sheep. Only our dear friend insisted we should come.

ROMAINVILLE: Her health comes first, her health comes first!

THE MOTHER: Isn't he domineering? His friends must do what he says; he can't bear not to have them with him. When he knew he was coming here, he wouldn't rest until the child came too.

ROMAINVILLE: She looked extremely pale. I said to myself –

THE MOTHER: Yes; yes; and we forgive you because we know you do it out of friendship, just as you did when you made her learn to swim.

ROMAINVILLE [*increasingly embarrassed*]: Everybody should learn to swim.

THE MOTHER: He came to the baths himself to watch her, and one day he fell in without taking his clothes off!

ROMAINVILLE [*beside himself*]: Didn't I say so, doesn't that prove everybody should learn to swim? We've chattered quite enough; Hugo must be wanting to give Isabelle her instructions. And I know you'd like to see the carriages arriving. You can come up to my room; it faces north, but you can see everyone who comes to the door.

THE MOTHER: Yes, that's it, we'll leave together. Of course I'm burning with curiosity to know what the mystery's about, but Isabelle will tell me tomorrow. Come along, then. I shall hide away like a dilapidated old moth who's been told not to dance round the candles.

ROMAINVILLE [*hurrying her off*]: That's right. Like a dilapidated old moth. Off we go. I can hear the first carriages arriving already.

HUGO: And you shall have supper brought up to you.

THE MOTHER: Just a crust, a crust and a glass of water for poor little Cinders. Enjoy yourself, you fortunate girl. I was twenty once; and not so long ago either . . . She looks charming, charming!

[*She goes, dragged off by* ROMAINVILLE.]

HUGO: And she's blushing.

ISABELLE: With embarrassment.

HUGO: Needlessly.

ISABELLE: It's easy enough to talk. My cheeks burn, my eyes are stinging, I've a lump in my throat, and I should like to be dead.

HUGO: She amuses me.

ISABELLE: She might amuse me, too, if only – [*She stops herself.*]

HUGO: If you had ever listened to what they call a society woman trying to put up the bidding for her daughter, you wouldn't be indignant any more. Your mother's discretion itself.

ISABELLE: I'm not plump, nor a skinnygalee; I've not got very good legs. I don't want to stay here.

HUGO: You can't go yet.

ISABELLE: I feel so ashamed.

HUGO: Why should you be? Because this party and the slight air of mystery has kindled your mother's imagination? Because she likes to think I'm in love with you and tries to throw you at my head? It's most natural. I'm rich, I belong to an old family, and ever since I was marriageable I've heard mothers hammering out that old tune. If you're ashamed because of me, forget your blushes. I've heard the tune so often, I'm deaf to it.

ISABELLE: But I can still hear it.

HUGO: Yes, I can see it must be unpleasant for you. I'm sorry.

ISABELLE [*suddenly*]: Have you considered Romainville?

HUGO: Oh no, I never do that. Romainville is scrupulous and considerate, but not considerable. I met you with him in a cake-shop at St Fleur. I thought you were charming, and it occurred to me you might be very useful this evening. That's all.

ISABELLE: But I think you should know . . .

HUGO: I don't want to know anything else at all.

ISABELLE [*softly, flatly*]: I see. I only wanted to – to tell you . . . Oh dear, I'm silly! I've been crying, and now I shall have to begin my face all over again. Will you excuse me for a little while?

HUGO: Of course.

[*She goes.* HUGO *signals to* JOSHUA *who is crossing the stage.*] Joshua!

JOSHUA: Mr Hugo!

HUGO: Does anyone suspect anything?

JOSHUA: No one, sir. The dress-shop people and the shoe-shop person have went, sir, unobserved. So many outside individuals here tonight, in any case, making the preparations . . .

HUGO: You'll keep your eye on the mother.

JOSHUA: As far as the human eye can be kept, sir. I beg your pardon, but she escaped my notice just now. What with all the responsibility for the Ball as well, sir . . .

HUGO: If only she'll content herself with trotting between here and her room, it may be all right. But she'll worry me considerably once the evening has really begun. [*He locks an imaginary door with a key.*] Click, click!

JOSHUA: Very good, sir. But if the lady starts to scream? We have to look all eventualities in the face, sir.

HUGO: Tell her I told you to shut her in, and promise her two hundred francs extra.

JOSHUA: Certainly, sir . . . Excuse me, sir, but . . . you think that will be sufficient to – to quench this particular individual, sir?

HUGO: Quite sufficient.

JOSHUA: Very good, sir.

[*To* ISABELLE *who re-enters as* JOSHUA *goes.*]

HUGO: Everything all right again?

ISABELLE: Yes; no sign of tears now.

HUGO: It's very useful to be able to disappear and come back with new eyes and a fresh smile, ready to pick up the conversation where you left off. The poor naked face of the male has to fight for a façade as best it can. [*He looks at his watch.*] It's almost ten o'clock: your dress makes you look like Helen of Troy: the first carriages are grinding the gravel in the drive: the fiddlers are rubbing rosin on their bows: and it's time I explained things to you.

ISABELLE: High time!

HUGO: I had to get to know you a little first. If you had been a fool I should have thought up a story for you, something picturesque and sentimental, a snip for a housewife's magazine. I'd begun to invent something like that when I asked you to come here. Something conventional; that's always the easiest. But, once in a very great while, something conventional is too threadbare for the circumstances, and a man's left standing stupidly with his intelligence on his arm, like a rolled umbrella he hadn't expected to use. So much the worse for me. Now I shall have to talk without preparation.

ISABELLE: I'm so sorry.

HUGO: Not at all. It's my fault for being such a poor judge of character. I ought to have been able to tell at a glance. You're not a fool, you have simplicity; you're not romantic, you're tender; you're not hard, you're exacting. Each one is almost like the other, but in fact they're opposites. This will teach me to look carelessly at girls in cake-shops! I'd thought of everything except one. I didn't expect you to look at me with such penetrating eyes.

ISABELLE: If it upsets you I can shut them.

HUGO: No, it's all right; your penetration will save time. I can cut the preamble and get to the point. Now, listen. I have a brother who is addled with love for a rich, young, beautiful girl. This party is in her honour.

ISABELLE: And she doesn't love him?

HUGO: She's engaged to him, which means that she gives him her lips two or three times a day, and no doubt lets him have contact occasionally with her pretty, lukewarm hand, while she turns her mind to something else. She makes all the loving gestures expected of her, she even tells him she loves him, but she doesn't.

ISABELLE: Does she love someone else?

HUGO: I should say she's quite incapable of loving anybody. But as she's a little multi-millionairess, and badly spoilt, blown sky-high by every breeze of a whim, she's made herself believe – yes, that she loves someone else.

ISABELLE: And that person is . . .

HUGO: As you've so quickly guessed, myself. You'll tell me she must be extremely stupid, because my brother is at least a thousand times nicer than I am.

ISABELLE: What does he look like?

HUGO: You see, that's the devil of preparing speeches in advance. I've forgotten to tell you the most important thing. We're twins.

ISABELLE: You look like each other.

HUGO: Physically, we're so alike it's neither permissible nor proper. But morally – morally, we're as different as day and night. My brother is good, sensible, kind, and intelligent, and I'm the reverse. But nevertheless she loves me and not him.

ISABELLE: And you?

HUGO: I?

ISABELLE: You love her, perhaps?

HUGO: I love nobody. That's why I can organize this evening's little comedy with complete serenity. I'm acting providence tonight. I deflect the influence of the stars! The stars, twinkling up there, without an inkling of what's going to happen tonight. Now this is what I want you to do.

ISABELLE: Tell me.

HUGO: To begin with, unquestioning obedience, and keep your eye on me all the time. I can only give you the broad outline; the details will have to be worked out as the evening goes on. Don't be afraid, you'll never be alone. I shall appear from behind a screen; I shall be behind the sofa where you go to sit with your partner, or under the tablecloth, or lurking in a shadow in the garden. I shall be everywhere, always watching you and whispering my orders to you. It's very simple. All you've got to do is to become the centre of interest; the party must revolve round you and no one else.

ISABELLE: You're expecting too much of me. I can never do it!

HUGO: I can do it. Don't worry, be yourself. Say whatever you want to say. Laugh whenever you want to laugh. If you suddenly feel like being alone, be alone. I shall expound you brilliantly; I shall make everything you say or do seem enchantingly extravagant and witty. I shall make them all think I'm in love with you.

ISABELLE [happily]: Will you?

HUGO: And you will make them all think you're in love with my brother.

ISABELLE: But if your brother is in love with this other girl, he won't even look at me!

HUGO: Being a fool, perhaps he won't. But even if he never takes his eyes off Diana *her* eyes will tell him that you're the beauty of the evening. She will be *so* jealous.

ISABELLE: It will make your brother love her more than ever.

HUGO: You think so? What a pretty idea of love you have in the theatre! No, put your mind at rest; I have everything nicely worked out. My brother is going to love you. It's all a question of waking him up. Diana isn't remotely the sort of girl he would want to love.

36

He's suffering in his sleep, walking along a parapet of infatuation, and we're going to waken him.

ISABELLE: Suppose he should die of it?

HUGO: Whoever died of love?

[ROMAINVILLE *enters, full spate.*]

ROMAINVILLE: There you are, there you are! I've been looking everywhere for you! Catastrophe!

HUGO: What do you mean, catastrophe?

ROMAINVILLE: My dear boy, the whole idea's exploded. Thank God!

HUGO: What are you talking about?

ROMAINVILLE: I was shepherding your mother back to her room, relying on the corridors being fairly dark, and we turned a corner slap into the Capulat!

ISABELLE: Capulat?

ROMAINVILLE: His aunt's companion.

HUGO: Well, you could pass that off all right.

ROMAINVILLE: I passed right on. But what did they do? They threw themselves like a pair of idiots into each other's arms, and burst into tears. It seems that they took piano-lessons together at the Mauberge Conservatoire. They've been thinking each other dead for twenty years, but, astonishing as it may be, they're alive! I was completely helpless. They're there still, looped around each other's necks, telling their life-stories. Thank God they're both talking at once, and neither knows what the other one's talking about. Whatever happens, there's only one thing for it: flight! [*To* ISABELLE.] Go up and change. I shall say you've been taken ill, you've had a telegram, your grandmother's had a stroke; I'll say something or other. I've got an imagination too. There's not a minute to lose. Go up and change!

HUGO: Stay down here. I forbid you to go.

[THE MOTHER *knocks and enters.*]

THE MOTHER: Coo-ee! Have you heard *my* little piece of excitement?

HUGO [*going to her*]: Yes. What have you been saying to her?

THE MOTHER: Oh, my dears, what bliss there can be in a friendship! You've often heard me speak of Geraldine Capulat, haven't you, Isabelle? I thought she was dead: but she's alive, the dear sweet soul. What have I been saying to her? Why, everything, everything, you know: my unhappy marriage, the end of my artistic career:

in fact, all my disappointments. You don't *know* what Geraldine has been to me! Both of us with golden hair; we were always taken for sisters.

HUGO: How did you explain your being in this house?

THE MOTHER: Quite simply. Did you think I should be taken off my guard? I told her I was one of the orchestra.

HUGO ⎫
ROMAINVILLE ⎭ Ouf!

THE MOTHER: But she didn't believe me. It wasn't a fortunate choice. It appears they are all negroes. So then do you know what I did? I have complete confidence in Geraldine. I made her swear on our long friendship that she wouldn't say a word to anybody, and I told her everything.

HUGO ⎫
ROMAINVILLE ⎭ [*in a panic*]: Everything?

THE MOTHER: Everything!

HUGO: How could you have told her everything? You know nothing about it.

THE MOTHER: No, but you know I'm quick with my little romances; like a big child, really; I'm incorrigible. I embroidered something to suit the case, a little figment!

ROMAINVILLE: A little figment?

HUGO: What little figment?

THE MOTHER: A little rosy-coloured figment! Oh dear, I believe you're going to scold me.

HUGO: Let's get to the point: what exactly have you said?

THE MOTHER: Nothing; just foolishness, words, day-dreams. I said you were in love with my little girl, and you wanted to bring her here without a lot of to-do, so you were pretending she was Mr Romainville's niece.

ISABELLE [*distressed*]: What right had you to say so?

ROMAINVILLE: Good heavens! My dear Hugo, by now your aunt knows the whole thing. I don't know what you're going to do, but I'm leaving. It's a great pity, I shall never be able to come here again. Our whole life gets altered by accidents! Go upstairs and change, for goodness' sake!

HUGO [*starting for the door*]: I shall have to find Capulat. We must make sure she keeps her mouth shut.

[*At the door he runs into* MME DESMERMORTES *pushed in her wheelchair by* CAPULAT. ROMAINVILLE *and* ISABELLE *hide* THE MOTHER *as well as they can.*]

MME DESMER: Where are you off to, Hugo, dear?

HUGO: Nowhere in particular.

MME DESMER: Then stop behaving like a cul-de-sac. I've come to see my young guest. Why hide her away in this hole and corner? I congratulate you, my dear friend.

ROMAINVILLE [*with a start, suspiciously*]: Congratulate me? Why congratulate me?

MME DESMER: She's very charming.

ROMAINVILLE: No!

MME DESMER: No?

ROMAINVILLE: Yes!

MME DESMER: Is she well and happy?

ROMAINVILLE: No – not just now. Rather faint.

MME DESMER: What nonsense are you talking? Her cheeks are like roses. One dance will put her on top of the world.

ROMAINVILLE [*not knowing what he's saying*]: She's afraid of getting a telegram.

MME DESMER: That's a curious anxiety. She's wearing such a pretty dress. Is that your present to her, you generous man?

ROMAINVILLE: Certainly not!

MME DESMER: I hope you like your room, my dear. Tomorrow morning you'll get the very first of the sunshine. Do you mean to enjoy yourself this evening?

ISABELLE: Oh yes!

MME DESMER: Who was it told me it was your first ball?

ROMAINVILLE: It wasn't I!

MME DESMER: Was it you, Hugo? No, it couldn't have been; you don't know her. I hope someone has introduced you?

HUGO: Yes, Aunt, someone has introduced us.

MME DESMER: She's entrancing, isn't she?

HUGO: Entrancing.

MME DESMER: Why don't you ask her to dance? They're playing the first waltz.

HUGO: I was about to. [*To* ISABELLE]: Will you give me the pleasure of this waltz, mademoiselle?

[*They waltz away together.* HUGO *drops a word to* ROMAINVILLE *as he goes past him.*]

She's bluffing. She doesn't know a thing.

ROMAINVILLE: She knows everything.

MME DESMER [*watching them go*]: She is exquisite, she is pretty, and she's well bred. How is it, Romainville, you've never talked about her to me?

ROMAINVILLE [*unhappily*]: I don't know . . . I can't explain it at all . . . not even – not even to myself.

MME DESMER [*signing to* CAPULAT *to push her towards the ball*]: Let me think, now: on her mother's side, if my memory serves, she is a Dandinet-Dandaine?

ROMAINVILLE: Yes, but . . .

MME DESMER: Then she's connected with the Rochemarsouins?

ROMAINVILLE: Perhaps, perhaps, but . . .

MME DESMER: If she's connected with the Rochemarsouins, she must also be a Cazaubon.

ROMAINVILLE: Yes, I suppose she must, but . . .

MME DESMER: My poor Antony was a Cazaubon through the Marsusses and the Villevilles, so he would have been as it were a slight relation of hers if he had lived.

ROMAINVILLE: As it were . . . but as it is, he is dead!

MME DESMER: But I'm still alive, Romainville, and I like to be quite clear about relationships. It's very important I should see exactly how this girl fits in. Now, let me see: you said her mother, who was a Fripont-Minet, is dead.

ROMAINVILLE: Dead!

MME DESMER: Her mother's cousin, then, one of the Laboulasses . . .

ROMAINVILLE [*interrupting*]: Also dead.

MME DESMER: The elder? The one I went to school with? I don't mean the younger one.

ROMAINVILLE: Dead, dead!

MME DESMER: What, both of them?

ROMAINVILLE: Both of them.

MME DESMER: And on her father's side: the Dupont-Pitard family?

ROMAINVILLE: All dead.

MME DESMER: Poor little thing! Why, she's living in a morgue!

ROMAINVILLE: A charnel-house!

[*They go.*]

[*As* CAPULAT *goes she drops her long mauve scarf.* THE MOTHER *comes out of hiding as cautiously as a great mouse. Re-enter* CAPULAT. *She rushes to* THE MOTHER.]

CAPULAT: I told them I had lost my scarf!

[*They fall into each other's arms.*]

THE MOTHER: To see you! To think that I really see you! It's like a dream!

CAPULAT: It is, isn't it, it really is! The whole thing, the whole thing's such a romance, it really is.

THE MOTHER: He worships her; you could see it in every look he gave!

CAPULAT: He's absurdly rich. It really is a romance!

THE MOTHER: And handsome as a lion! You must help me, my dear, or my little girl will die of it.

CAPULAT: I'll do anything and everything. The whole thing's such a romance, it really is. Ah, dear! Our little wild whirling days at Mauberge, can you remember them? The cake-shop Marius Laubonne!

THE MOTHER: And the ice-creams at Pinteau's!

CAPULAT: And the first duet we played together, at the Charity Concert for the Mauberge Widows' Fund! [*She listens to the music.*] The 'Invitation Waltz'.

THE MOTHER: The 'Invitation Waltz'. [*She starts to sing the music.*] La, si, do, re, do, la, sol, la, sol, fa, mi, re, do.

[*The orchestra takes up the waltz during the final bar and continues playing.* THE MOTHER *and* CAPULAT *stand for a moment rocking to and fro, with their heads together, then* CAPULAT *breaks away and creeps furtively off, blowing kisses with her scarf.*

THE MOTHER, *her eyes half closed, her head leaning on her hands, starts to waltz herself.* JOSHUA *appears, moves towards her like a man stalking a butterfly.*

She goes out waltzing without seeing him. He follows her.]

CURTAIN

ACT TWO

Behind the lowered curtain, gay music of the dance.

As the curtain rises, couples are whirling round the stage; the music comes to an end, and they drift away. MADAME DESMERMORTES *enters in her wheel-chair, pushed by* CAPULAT.

CAPULAT [*after a pause*]: Well, the ball has really got going now, hasn't it, madam?

MME DESMER [*peevishly*]: It can get going and go, for all I care. It bores me until I don't know whether to yawn or yelp. I was never fond of dancing, and since I've been screwed to this chair, it looks more than ever like the hopping of kangaroos. You've never liked it either, have you?

CAPULAT [*simpering*]: I was a girl of twenty, you know, once upon a time.

MME DESMER: When, for goodness' sake? You've never looked any different to me.

CAPULAT: Oh yes, I was, madam. I was young when I was with the Baron and Baroness, before I came here.

MME DESMER: Ah, well you may have thought so. You're a nice girl, Capulat, but . . . you know this as well as I do . . . you're plain. No one who is plain can ever have been twenty.

CAPULAT: But a heart beats in my breast all the same, madam.

MME DESMER: My good soul, a heart with no face is more bother than everything else put together. Let's talk no more about it . . . you've been quite happy, Capulat, without a face; you've been respected and you've been appreciated. What could be nicer than that?

CAPULAT: On evenings like this, when there's music and the young people dancing under the chandeliers, I feel something indescribable in the air.

MME DESMER: Then don't attempt to describe it. It's much too late. You really have nothing to grumble about. And there's always the life to come. A dull life in this world is a splendid recommendation for the next.

CAPULAT: Oh, madam.

MME DESMER: You will be hobnobbing with the Blessed while I'm roasting over a slow fire for two or three thousand years. Well, perhaps it won't seem so long.

CAPULAT: God's mercy is infinite, madam.

MME DESMER: Certainly; but He must abide by what He says, you know, otherwise the Just like you, who've staked everything on it, are going to feel very badly let down. Suppose a rumour started circulating among the Sheep that the Goats were going to be pardoned as well? They would use such bad language that they'd get themselves damned on the spot. Don't you think it would be rather comic?

CAPULAT: Oh, you can't really think that, madam!

MME DESMER: Why not? I can think anything I like, it's all I have to do ... Push me nearer the doors where I can see the frisking of little fools. Isn't that Romainville's niece dancing with my nephew?

CAPULAT: Yes, madam.

MME DESMER: She has a very unusual grace; the only woman who is being herself. Why didn't Romainville bring her here before?

CAPULAT: She's so graceful, really she is, isn't she? She has such ... what shall I say ...?

MME DESMER: Whatever you care to, dear; I'm not listening. Do you know what I think? I think you'll need amusing this evening. Now, what can we think of to liven ourselves up?

CAPULAT: A cotillion?

MME DESMER: A cotillion! That is so like you! You couldn't have suggested anything sillier. Except the ball itself ... Look at them twirling and twiddling! They think they're enjoying themselves, but all they're doing is twizzling their vain little heads. The world isn't amusing any more; it's time I left it. The fabulous evenings I've known in my time. In 1902, for instance, at Biarritz, the Duke of Medino-Solar was out-of-this-world in love with the Countess Funela. You won't guess what he did. They were giving a public assembly – a ridotto, it used to be called – and everyone had to be dressed in yellow. Well, the Duke came in green! It was the colour of his mistress's eyes, but of course nobody understood that. The rules of a ridotto were always very strict, and they refused to let him in. The Duke was a Spaniard of the hottest and bluest blood. Without any attempt to explain, he killed the footman. Of course, the ball went on. Their Highnesses the Infantas were there, so it was decided that anonymity should still be respected. The police were brought in, wearing yellow dominoes, and if you happened to dance with them you could see their beady eyes and really horrible moustaches under their masks. But, as they could only dance with the ladies, they weren't able to spot the Duke! The next day he crossed the frontier and a bull killed him in Madrid. That's what living used to be!

CAPULAT: Yes, of course, but one doesn't know, really one doesn't; romantic things may be going on here, at this very moment.

MME DESMER: At this ball? Dear Capulat, you should go and lie down.

CAPULAT: Perhaps so, but perhaps not so. Suppose there was a young, rich, handsome man, spellbound with love, who had smuggled his loved one into the ball . . . But I've said too much. I promised I wouldn't breathe a word.

MME DESMER: Why should I suppose there was?

CAPULAT: And, as well as the young man, an old friend, a dear, dear friend given up for dead, suddenly coming back like the bluebells in May! It's really wonderful, it really is, suddenly to take part in a fairy story!

MME DESMER: Bluebells? Fairy story? Capulat, I don't know what you're talking about.

CAPULAT: To think the world is still so colourful, madam, it really is! Love can still be stronger than social barriers, careless of scandal, as pure as death. There can still be the desperate plot, the impersonation, madam. And the poor apprehensive mother, hiding herself away and watching her child's triumph without ever . . . ever . . . Oh, I really can't stop the tears, madam, I can't really. I'm so sorry!

MME DESMER: Suppose you explain yourself, Capulat, instead of watering my hair? What apprehensive mother, what impersonations?

CAPULAT: Oh, I've said too much! I promised I wouldn't breathe a word!

MME DESMER: A word about what?

CAPULAT: It's a secret, madam; the diamond at the bottom of a mine. She loves him, he worships her, she is poor, he brings her here disguised. It's really like a fairy story, really it is, isn't it?

MME DESMER: She? He? Who are these people?

CAPULAT: Everyone is either whispering her name or asking who she is. She moves among them like a queen. Her evening of triumph! And her mother played the treble and I played the bass, all those years ago . . . I'm so sorry; do forgive me; it's all too much!

MME DESMER: Capulat, you've been my companion for twenty years, and though you've never said anything that amused me I've always been able to understand you. At last you interest me and I can't understand a word. Either you explain, or you leave my service.

CAPULAT: Oh, I've said too much! I promised not to breathe a word. I'd rather die in poverty; I'd rather you killed me!

MME DESMER: I wouldn't dream of it. I'm used to being obeyed without having to kill people. And you know I always give you my old clothes. Don't I deserve a little consideration?

CAPULAT: I know, I know that, madam! I'm being nearly torn apart by the two duties. Oh, madam, we were such friends, we both played on the same piano! Such happy days! I thought she was dead and I found her again. She told me she belonged to the orchestra, but they were all negroes. I was astonished. Then she confided in me, and swore me to secrecy. All about the mad love of this young man for her daughter, and the stratagem of the good kind friend.

MME DESMER: What good kind friend?

CAPULAT: M. Guy-Charles Romainville, such a good kind man!

MME DESMER: What has he done?

CAPULAT: His niece is not his niece. Love snaps its fingers! A young man who is very close to you. But I've said too much. I promised not to breathe a word.

MME DESMER: Promised whom?

CAPULAT: My dearest friend. I promised on the days of our duets. So better to die! . . . Oh, madam, the violins! They're like strong wine to me!

MME DESMER: So I've noticed, mon amie! Push me to my room where we shan't hear them, and tell me the rest of it.

CAPULAT: You're so good, madam; there's nothing you can't do! A word from you, and all the obstacles will evaporate.

MME DESMER: Well, we shall see about that. Trundle me off and explain things without falling over yourself. You were saying that Romainville's niece . . .

CAPULAT: Is not his niece, madam. She's your nephew's loved one. He wanted her to be the belle of the ball. So he had a dress brought from Paris for her, and he begged her mother, my dear, sweet friend . . .

MME DESMER: My nephew? Which nephew? Frederic?

CAPULAT: No, madam. Mr Hugo. But, oh dear, I'm sure I've said too much! I promised not to breathe a word . . .

[*They go.*

The music wells up again. Enter LADY INDIA *and* PATRICE BOMBELLES, *dancing a Mexican tango.*]

PATRICE: They've put me in a room looking out on the park, facing direct north . . . it's most unkind . . . and they've moved all my things, in the middle of the afternoon, without telling me. They said they couldn't find me, but they're not going to make me believe that. I never left the billiard-room. They couldn't find me because they didn't want to find me.

LADY INDIA: Then who has got your room?

PATRICE: Romainville's niece. The girl with the lovely eyes. But that's only the excuse. The real reason is that he saw us together yesterday, and wants to have me farther away from your room.

LADY INDIA: Nonsense! He would have to explain it all to my aunt. You mustn't be idiotic. And how do you know she has lovely eyes?

PATRICE: Who, dear heart?

LADY INDIA: This niece of Romainville's.

PATRICE: Have I said so?

LADY INDIA: Now be careful, Patrice, I don't like competitors. And if Messerschmann *has* seen us together and feels like braining you, I shall quite understand. Frankly, Patrice, I should be very disappointed if he didn't. Don't you agree?

PATRICE: Well, I suppose . . . I don't know . . . I suppose so.

LADY INDIA: I may deceive Messerschmann, but I like to think well of him. The man I love must be noble and courageous, and the man I deceive must be noble and courageous too. It gives life a kind of dignity which is most pleasing. Surely, Patrice, you, so proud and susceptible, would be terribly upset if he didn't give a savage cry of uncontrollable jealousy?

PATRICE: I – well, Dorothy, I –

LADY INDIA: Exactly! Men of your calibre wouldn't want a woman who wasn't fiercely loved already. Creatures such as ourselves have no patience with the lukewarm. We blaze! Other people may be born to live, but we're on earth to blaze.

PATRICE: Yes, Dorothy.

LADY INDIA: And it's very nice of us to bother about him at all. Suppose he does ruin us? What fun it would be to be poor, as long as one was *excessively* poor! Anything in excess is most exhilarating.

PATRICE: Yes, Dorothy!

LADY INDIA: Our squalor would seem like a great dark poem, wouldn't it, Patrice?

PATRICE: Very dark!

LADY INDIA: How amusing it would be! I should wash the dishes and clean the flues, whatever that may be, and bake and brew. How beautifully I should brew! I must ask Roeseda Soeurs to make me some affecting little aprons. There's no one else, you know, who so well understands my style. What miracles she will do with a scrap of muslin and a ruche! And then I shall set to work with my tiny dustbin and my tiny broom. And you will work in a factory. I know so many people on the Steel Board; they'll find you a job as a metal-worker easily. You will come home in the evening, nearly dead with fatigue, and smelling dreadfully. It will be absolutely delicious! And I shall wash you down, my dear, from head to foot with a tiny sponge. It's beautiful to be poor, Patrice.

PATRICE: Beautiful?

LADY INDIA: Let him come. What is he waiting for? His money is burning my fingers. I shall give it all back, immediately, everything except the pearls.

[MESSERSCHMANN *enters and stops, not daring to approach.*]

PATRICE [*terrified*]: Do be careful – he's here! Do be careful!

LADY INDIA: Don't be such a coward, Patrice!

PATRICE: I don't like you. I've never liked you. I'm never likely to like you.

LADY INDIA: What?

PATRICE: I'm only with you out of sheer necessity. It's quite obvious you bore me. Anyone can see that I'm yawning. [*He yawns.*]

LADY INDIA: Patrice, don't dare to yawn! Take my arm. We'll go away, dancing as ostentatiously as possible.

PATRICE: You're crazy!

LADY INDIA: When the bull is drowsy, one stirs it up with a banderilla. [*Aloud, as they dance off.*] Have you ever seen a bull-fight, dear friend?

PATRICE [*aloud*]: Yes, dear friend, but I didn't like it.

LADY INDIA [*aside to him*]: Hold your head up. Don't look as though we've seen him. He needn't know yet we know he knows.

PATRICE [*stumbling in tongue and foot*]: Yes, but perhaps he doesn't know, Dorothy. Don't you think that by seeming to know we know he knows we run the risk of making him know?

[*They go.* MESSERSCHMANN *makes to follow them. He calls* JOSHUA, *who is crossing the stage.*]

MESSER: Come here, my friend!

JOSHUA: Sir?

MESSER: The two people walking along the terrace there; they'd be making for the greenhouses, I suppose?

JOSHUA: Yes, sir. Would you care to give me your order for supper, sir?

MESSER: Noodles.

JOSHUA: Without butter, sir?

MESSER: And without salt.

JOSHUA: Very good, sir.

MESSER [*makes to go, then hesitates*]: Tell me, my friend . . .

JOSHUA: Sir?

MESSER: If I go down those steps, I get to the greenhouses through the orchard, do I not?

JOSHUA: Yes, sir. But if you are hoping to catch up with the lady and gentleman, sir, I take the liberty to say that I've been watching the lady and gentleman, sir, while you were giving me your order, and they've come back into the house by the small door at the end of the terrace. The lady and gentleman have no doubt gone upstairs by the little staircase, sir.

MESSER: I see!

JOSHUA: No doubt they wish to tidy their persons up, as it were, sir.

48

MESSER [*sighing*] : No doubt yes. Thank you.

[*He is going out when* JOSHUA *bows and says*] :

JOSHUA: Without butter?

MESSER [*sighing, sombrely*] : And without salt.

[*He goes,* JOSHUA *also.*

    Couples, waltzing, fill the stage again. FREDERIC *crosses thoughtfully among the crowd of dancers.* ISABELLE *enters. At the end of the dance* FREDERIC *re-enters, still searching, through another door. He sees* ISABELLE. *They stand, looking at one another, a little uncomfortably, on the now empty stage.*]

ISABELLE: I hope you'll forgive me?

FREDERIC: For what, mademoiselle?

ISABELLE: I must seem to be following you. I happened to come in here and . . . and found you were here before me.

FREDERIC: Yes, of course.

ISABELLE: I'm enjoying . . . enjoying the evening very much.

FREDERIC: Yes, it's splendid.

[*A silence. We hear the orchestra playing. They don't know what to say to one another.*]

That's a very pretty dress you're wearing.

ISABELLE: Yes, it is pretty. [*Another silence, and then she suddenly asks*] : Do you believe in them, I wonder?

FREDERIC: Believe in them?

ISABELLE: In ghosts.

FREDERIC: A little. Why?

ISABELLE: You look as though you might be your brother's ghost, made very sad by something.

FREDERIC: It's what I am.

ISABELLE: You're young, you're handsome, and you're rich. What can possibly have made you sad?

FREDERIC: Being handsome, as you call it, being young and rich, and nothing to be gained by it. Will you excuse me if I leave you now?

ISABELLE: Yes, certainly.

[FREDERIC *goes into the garden.*

    A snatch from the orchestra, perhaps. HUGO *bursts in through another door.*]

HUGO: That was perfect!

ISABELLE: I didn't know what to say. I feel very shy with him.

HUGO: Excellent!

ISABELLE: He'll wonder why I'm always at his elbow, and why I keep trying to speak to him.

HUGO: That's what I want.

ISABELLE [*sinking into a chair*]: I can't do it any more.

HUGO [*sternly*]: We're not yet past midnight, and you have a duty till dawn. Up you get! You're a kindly creature, and this is a kindly action you're doing. I can promise you won't regret it. That's right; look at him just as you're looking now. You're an astonishing actress. Where did you learn that look of deep regard?

ISABELLE: It's my own.

HUGO: Congratulations. Turn it on Frederic from now till morning. He couldn't help being moved by it.

ISABELLE [*softly*]: It may be different when it turns on him.

HUGO: Well, something in the same line will do. Dear little brother; he's not used to being given pretty looks. Look out, he's coming back. He wants to talk to you after all, you see. Now, compose yourself and use your imagination. I shall be listening.

[*He disappears.* FREDERIC *returns.*]

FREDERIC: My brother was looking for you just now.

ISABELLE: Oh, was he?

FREDERIC: Usually, when my brother is looking for a girl she knows it.

ISABELLE: Oh, I . . . I didn't know.

FREDERIC: He's very good-looking; don't you think so?

ISABELLE: Yes – very.

FREDERIC: We're as alike as two blades of grass, but it's only men who get us confused. Women always know which is my brother. How do they do it?

ISABELLE: I don't know.

FREDERIC: It's because he doesn't look at them, maybe. That's a very pretty dress you're wearing.

ISABELLE: Isn't it? He's not only good-looking.

FREDERIC: Who?

ISABELLE: Your brother.

FREDERIC: No. He's very intelligent; much more intelligent than I am. Very brave, too; completely fearless; always ready to shoot the rapids or put his hand in the fire. But there's one thing he couldn't ever do, not every day for any length of time. He couldn't be in love; and perhaps that's why they love him. He's very hard, but he's also very kind.

ISABELLE: He's very fond of you. He wouldn't like to see you hurt.

FREDERIC: It would irritate him. It's not so much that he's very fond of me. It annoys him to see me unhappy. He doesn't like people to be unhappy. Particularly unhappy in love. [*He gets up.*] Honestly, he's looking for you. I'm looking for someone, too. If I come across him during my search shall I tell him where you are?

ISABELLE: Really, no. Thank you, but don't tell him.

FREDERIC: He's good company; much more so than I am.

ISABELLE: I like being with you. Please stay!

[*FREDERIC looks at her in astonishment and sits beside her with a sigh.*]

FREDERIC: Oh! How sad it all is!

ISABELLE: How sad all what is?

FREDERIC: I'm sorry. What I'm going to say isn't very polite. Perhaps it's impolite, though I don't want to be impolite. But if the girl I'm looking for so unsuccessfully had said what you have just said I might very well have died of happiness.

ISABELLE [*smiling nicely at him*]: Then it's as well that it was I who said it. [*She gets up.*] And it wasn't in the least impolite. I understand how you feel only too well.

FREDERIC [*also rising*]: Thank you for understanding, but forgive me all the same, and forgive me if I go now.

ISABELLE: Of course.

FREDERIC: Good-bye.

[*He goes.* HUGO *enters immediately, by the same door, in a bad temper.*]

HUGO: No, no, no! I didn't bring you here for that!

ISABELLE: What have I done?

HUGO: Sighing and hinting that you'd rather be with someone else! No more of that! You're paid to act a part, my dear, so act it. And without being ashamed of it. It's a serious job, and you should try to do it well.

ISABELLE [*gently*]: Please don't go on.

HUGO: Why?

ISABELLE: If you went on talking to me in that voice, I should cry.

HUGO: Now that really would be a good idea. I wouldn't have suggested it myself. Manufactured tears always look a bit grotesque; but if you'll cry naturally, excellent! My dear little brother will founder at once!

ISABELLE: Why haven't you a heart?

HUGO: Because my brother has too much. We were born at the same time, and things were divided between us, this and that to me, a heart to him.

ISABELLE: But you must be able to see that I'm unhappy?

HUGO: Splendidly. You have a way of being unhappy that would fetch tears out of a rock. Have you a twin-sister, by any chance, without a heart?

ISABELLE: I can't bear you!

HUGO: It's a very good thing you can't. Tell my brother so, and swim away with him in a flood of sympathy. That's just what I want.

ISABELLE: You don't suppose I'm doing what I'm told this evening just for the sake of this dress and a fee for dancing?

HUGO: My pretty one, I thought nothing so unpleasant.

ISABELLE: I'm not interested in your brother, or in curing him, or in looking well-dressed, or in having everyone looking at me. Men have looked at me before, even when I wasn't dressed well. Do you think that's amusing?

HUGO: Don't fight back the tears any more, let yourself go. Cry, cry, cry, my dear. That's better. You see how easy it is.

ISABELLE [crying]: Now my eyes will be red. Isn't that rather clever of me?

HUGO: Superbly! [He throws himself suddenly on his knees and declaims theatrically.] Ah! Isabelle, dear Isabelle! I suffer too, I die as well!

ISABELLE [stopping crying]: What are you doing?

HUGO: He's coming back. Stay just as you are. I want him to find me at your feet.

ISABELLE: Oh, no; this is dreadful!

HUGO [on his knees]: Yes, my darling. My heart is overflowing! I'm drowning in it. A heart in full flood! Is he coming towards us?

ISABELLE: Yes. Oh, please get up!

HUGO: Now's the time; all or nothing. Ah well; I suppose I'd better kiss you.

[He takes her in his arms and kisses her. She relaxes with a little cry – then she suddenly asks]:

ISABELLE: Why did you say 'Ah well'?

HUGO [*bowing coldly*]: You must excuse me. A kiss was necessary.
  [*He makes his escape. She drops to the sofa, crying.*]

FREDERIC [*entering*]: Are you crying?

ISABELLE: Yes.

FREDERIC: You ought to be happy; my brother kissed you. Usually when that happens, the girl is blushing and dancing like fire. But you're pale and you're crying.

ISABELLE: Yes.

FREDERIC: I'm sorry. Perhaps he went away because he saw me coming.

ISABELLE: No.

FREDERIC: Don't be unhappy. One unhappy person at a party is enough. I don't know how it is, but I should hate it if you were unhappy too.

ISABELLE: Please let me alone.

FREDERIC: I want to tell you something; I realize it's no consolation to hear other people's troubles, but even so. It's something I've been almost certain about since yesterday. She chose to be engaged to me because she couldn't be engaged to my brother. She said to herself, 'If the other one won't have me I'll take his double'.

ISABELLE: If that were true it would be shameful.

FREDERIC: No; very lucky, really. Otherwise she would never have chosen me at all. Anyway, I'm used to it. When we were small, if my brother was naughty and the governess couldn't find him, she punished me. It was a sort of alternative. Life only comes to me absent-mindedly.

ISABELLE: You, as well.

FREDERIC: Why do you say 'You, as well'? You can't know what it feels like. I don't mean to pay you an empty compliment, this is hardly the moment; but I'm certain no one could mistake you for anyone else.

  [ISABELLE *is looking off-stage, suddenly tense. She shakes her head to someone in the wings. Then*]:

ISABELLE: It wasn't because of your brother that I was crying.

FREDERIC: No?

ISABELLE: It was because of you.

FREDERIC: Because of me?

ISABELLE: Yes – Frederic, it's you I love.

FREDERIC: Oh!

[*He goes.*

   ISABELLE *runs across the stage;* HUGO *returns, dragging her by the hand.*]

HUGO: Very good! But you needn't have run away! That's the first time anyone has told him they loved him. You see, you've made him walk with quite a swagger! Let's make things even brisker. A pinch of jealousy while the blood's on the simmer. A third young man is in love with you.

ISABELLE: What young man?

HUGO: That's my business; I'll find one. Furious because I never leave your side, he challenges me to fight, and we choose our weapons.

ISABELLE: You're mad!

HUGO: Imagine it – a duel by moonlight, in the spinney, during supper. Conversation disrupted by the sound of pistol shots. They stop the orchestra, and all troop into the park with lanterns and hurricane lamps to look for the corpse. And then you, your wits crazed with love (you do understand you're crazed with love, don't you, Isabelle?) – you throw yourself into the lake. You swim, I imagine? Well, anyway, it doesn't matter; you've got feet, the lake's no depth, and I shall be there. I shall fish you out, carry you back to land, lay you streaming with water on the grass at my brother's feet, and say to him, 'There! You did this!' And if he doesn't love you after that he's got more resistance than I have . . . You're looking rather dubious. Don't you enjoy bathing? I'll treble your fee. I'll buy you another dress. [*He takes her in his arms before she can draw back; he suddenly speaks like a little spoilt boy.*] Be a nice girl, agree to it, to please me. I'm enjoying myself so much tonight, and it's not often that I do.

ISABELLE [*breaking away and running off with the same hurt cry as before*]: Oh!

DIANA [*entering suddenly*]: Frederic!

HUGO [*turning with a smile*]: Hugo, if you please.

DIANA: Oh! I beg your pardon.

HUGO: I'm not blushing. The one who doesn't blush is Hugo. Remember that: you may find it useful. Are you looking for him?

DIANA: I thought it was Frederic with that girl in his arms. As it was you, it's different. I apologize. Have you seen him?

HUGO: Of course. Everybody except you has seen him. He wanders like a soul in pain through this desert of gaiety. Why? Are you wanting to satisfy yourself that you've well and truly broken his heart this evening?

DIANA: I don't want to break anyone's heart. It wouldn't amuse me. [*She takes a step and stops.*] By the way, when I was in the park yesterday, one of you kissed me, and Frederic swears it wasn't him. I lied so that he shouldn't be upset. But it must have been you. It's the kind of joke I detest.

HUGO: Yesterday? In the park? At what time?

DIANA: Don't pretend not to remember, Hugo. After dinner.

HUGO: After dinner? You've made a mistake, my dear. I was playing billiards with Patrice Bombelles.

DIANA: Frederic swears it wasn't him.

HUGO: I can only suppose it was yet another son of Adam, making the most of some vague resemblance to us.

DIANA: You're wrong to play with your brother's feelings, Hugo; it's too cruel. Even if you loved me, even if your love for me were too strong to control. But it isn't too strong to control, is it?

HUGO: You put me in an impossible situation, Diana. I'm obliged to say No.

DIANA: I hate you!

HUGO: You, as well? I'm not very popular this evening. Have you seen Patrice Bombelles? I gather he's looking everywhere for me. It's funny, but he didn't take to finding me in that little girl's arms, either. It seems he's mad about her. I didn't know, though I suppose I might have guessed, because everybody seems to be. And I admit she's enchanting, and she's wearing a very pretty dress, moreover. Don't you find it so? Well, good-bye. Shall I send Frederic to you?

DIANA: Thank you all the same. I'll find him myself.

[*He goes.* DIANA *remains alone, unable to relax. Suddenly she calls for her father.*]

DIANA: Father!

MESSER: Well, dear?

DIANA: Did you hear him? Did you hear how he was mocking me?

MESSER: No, dear.

DIANA: Why not?

MESSER: Because I wasn't there.

DIANA: Things are going so wrong you'd think we had no money at all. Would you be so good as to make me happy again, at once?

MESSER: But what is the matter, my darling girl? You wanted this boy Frederic and I bought him for you. Is he trying to get out of it?

DIANA: You didn't buy him for me; he loves me. But his brother is laughing at me.

MESSER: I can't give you both of them; not because I'm not rich enough, but it isn't the custom. Marry whichever you prefer.

DIANA: You're not rich enough to buy me the one I prefer. That's why I took the other one.

MESSER: Not rich enough! Don't put me in a rage!

DIANA: Well, look what's happening to me, and it's Hugo who's making it happen, deliberately, I'm certain. I'm certain he brought this girl here, and she's trying to make Frederic lose interest in me; and Hugo, who never looks at anybody, the cold impersonal Hugo, never takes his eyes off her. I should begin to think I wasn't here, except that everyone has such an air of *not* looking at me that I know I must be. It's bad enough to be looked at as though you weren't there, but it's terrible, terrible, *not* to be looked at as though you were. So please set about making me happy again.

MESSER [*thoughtfully*]: Who is this girl? I can do almost nothing with a young girl.

DIANA: Romainville's niece.

MESSER: Which is Romainville?

DIANA: He's the one who looks as though he has gone on a horse to catch butterflies.

MESSER: But where does his money come from?

DIANA: He's a director of one of your companies, like all the rest of the men here.

MESSER: What does Romainville seem to be on? Steel, cement, potash, sulphates, zinc, aluminium, creosote, nuts, nickel, emulsion, tyres, bijouterie, sewing machines, tunnels, racquets . . .

DIANA: I think he said something about pig-iron.

MESSER: Pig-iron! Lead me to him. What do you want this Romainville to do, my darling girl? Do you want me to make him send her away at the height of the ball?

DIANA: Oh – do you think you can?

MESSER: I've got them all in the palm of my hand. I lift a finger and their incomes are only half as much.

DIANA: I'm afraid it's impossible, Father.

MESSER [*calmly*]: If he has a ha'penny in pig-iron, nothing is impossible.

[*He takes her by the hand and they go.*

Enter PATRICE *and* HUGO *from opposite sides. The orchestra plays a heroic, warlike tune.*]

HUGO: Sir?

PATRICE: Sir?

HUGO: I was looking for you.

PATRICE: For me?

HUGO: Yes. I want to speak to you.

PATRICE: About what?

HUGO: You were in the park yesterday, I think, with Lady Dorothy India, my cousin?

PATRICE: Possibly.

HUGO: I noticed you. You seemed to be having a rather heated discussion.

PATRICE: On quite general matters, if I remember.

HUGO: I don't doubt it. But at one moment you must have out-generalled yourself; the lady slapped your face.

PATRICE: Mine, sir?

HUGO: This one.

PATRICE: You're mistaken, sir.

HUGO: No, sir.

PATRICE: That is to say, the lady may have struck me, but that's no reason for you to think what you appear to be thinking, sir!

HUGO: What do I appear to be thinking?

PATRICE: After all, damn it, a slap on the cheek isn't always the sign of an understanding between a man and a woman.

HUGO: Certainly not.

PATRICE: One slaps the most casual acquaintances, even complete strangers. It proves absolutely nothing. For instance, if I suddenly struck you now, would you deduce from this that we were on amorous terms?

HUGO: I'd protect myself from that to the death!

PATRICE: Then may I ask why you're trying to provoke me? Winks, sighs, hints, unpleasant chuckles, which you try to camouflage with cigar-smoke? You didn't fool me yesterday on the terrace; oh no, I wasn't fooled for a moment.

HUGO: You're very clairvoyant.

PATRICE: I can't go on, I can't go on another hour!

HUGO: This is just what I wanted to make you say. [*He takes his arm.*] Let's talk it over quietly, like the nice fellows we are. I need your help. Between you and me and the bed-post, this long-drawn-out affair with my mad cousin is boring you to desperation – admit it!

PATRICE: I've never said so.

HUGO: Naturally not. But let's speak frankly, shall we? You're in the hell of a cleft stick. If Messerschmann gets to know she's your mistress . . .

PATRICE [*terrified*]: Don't say that, don't mention it!

HUGO: He'll break your neck!

PATRICE [*in a terrible state*]: I've been enduring this for two years, twenty-four months – a hundred and four nerve-racking weeks, seven hundred and twenty-eight days . . .

HUGO: Never mind, dear man; it will be all over this evening.

PATRICE: What do you mean?

HUGO: In the simplest possible way. Imagine you're on a visit to the dentist. You've rung the bell, flicked over the pages of the magazines in the waiting-room, and now you're sitting in the dentist's chair. You've shown him the bad tooth; the dentist has seized the forceps. You're a big boy now; it's too late to run off home.

PATRICE: Do you know my dentist?

HUGO: No.

PATRICE: What are you talking about?

HUGO: This! Either you fall in with my plans this evening, or else, to be honest with you, I make quite sure that your employer knows how you employ yourself.

PATRICE: No!

HUGO: Now I wonder what you mean when you say no?

PATRICE: You're a gentleman, you wouldn't do it.

HUGO: Not by an anonymous letter or by bribing a servant; but though I do things like a gentleman, I do them.

PATRICE: You're contemptible!

HUGO: I see.

PATRICE: And you're not ashamed?

HUGO: Not at all.

PATRICE: Oh. Then there's nothing more to discuss. What do you want me to do?

HUGO: I want you to choose the alternative way of having your neck broken. There's a very charming girl here tonight. It's a matter of the greatest importance, which I can't explain, that you should pretend you're desperately in love with her.

PATRICE: I?

HUGO: You. But that's not all. You've seen me in the arms of this girl, and in a fit of ungovernable jealousy you box my ears.

PATRICE: I?

HUGO: You. Come with me. We put the incident on a proper footing. We fight by moonlight, in the spinney, with pistols. Don't be afraid; I'm a very good shot. I promise I shan't hit you.

[*They go.*

Enter CAPULAT, *followed by* THE MOTHER, *magnificently dressed and plumed.*]

CAPULAT: Oh! Oh! You look like the best in the land, you do really, really, you do!

THE MOTHER: Do I, Capulat?

CAPULAT: Really you do! You couldn't look nicer in that dress if you'd been born in it!

THE MOTHER: It's my dreams come true, isn't it? I feel as if I'd been born in it.

CAPULAT: No one could doubt it. But wait, wait! I'll go and find madam.

[*As she goes,* JOSHUA *enters. He stops suddenly, rooted to the spot, when he sees* THE MOTHER *in her finery.*]

JOSHUA: Oh!

THE MOTHER: My man, would you kindly announce me? The Countess Funela.

JOSHUA: The countess . . .?

THE MOTHER [*magnificently*]: Funela!

JOSHUA [*goes out shouting*]: Mr Hugo! Help me, Mr Hugo, sir . . .!

[JOSHUA *goes out.*

Enter MME DESMERMORTES, *pushed by* CAPULAT. JOSHUA
goes past without seeing her.]

MME DESMER: Where's he running? What is it? Fire? That would be
most diverting ... Let me see you, *ma chérie! Mille tonnerres!* Why,
she's a great success! Now we'll go in and make a sensation.

[*Enter* HUGO *with* JOSHUA.]

My dear Hugo, I know you will be delighted to be presented to
one of my oldest and dearest friends. The Countess Funela. We
knew one another in Italy. My nephew, Hugo, Countess.

THE MOTHER: I'm so charmed to meet you!

HUGO: Madam!

MME DESMER: Come along, my dear; wheel me, Capulat. I'm so
happy to see you again after such a desolation of separation. We can
talk about Venice. Such days! Do you remember Palestrini? Such
a madman! Jaundice made an end of him. Now I shall introduce
you to all my other guests. Tell me, my dear, you have a daughter,
isn't that so? What has become of her?

THE MOTHER: Oh, it's a very long story indeed.

MME DESMER: Well, you must let me hear it. We have all the night
before us ...

[*They have gone.*]

JOSHUA [*badly shaken*]: Here's the key, Mr Hugo. So she can only
have got out through the window, unless madam opened the door
herself. The Countess Funela! When she said that, I could have
knocked myself down with one of her feathers. [*He so far forgets
himself as to sit down and quickly jumps up again.*] Oh, I beg your
pardon, sir.

HUGO: What for?

JOSHUA: I sat down. Quite an accident, sir. That hasn't happened to
me before in thirty years.

ROMAINVILLE [*entering*]: Stop! Oh, stop! Stop!

HUGO: Stop what?

ROMAINVILLE: Everything, stop everything! This time it's altogether
calamitous! We're fallen into a trap, we're caught by the avalanche!
High finance at its worst! Don't say a word about it! Isabelle must
be got away this instant, this very moment, or else I'm ruined!

HUGO: What in the world are you raving about? Everybody's out of
their minds tonight!

ROMAINVILLE: I'm a director of several sulphate companies, and one pig-iron company.

HUGO: Yes, we know that. But what's that got to do with it?

ROMAINVILLE: That's why Isabelle must leave this house at once! Yes: powerful financial interests make it essential! Not a word! I can't explain. Manoeuvres at the Stock Exchange. If you won't help me, your aunt can go to the devil. I'd sooner have the scandal. I'd sooner upset her for life. I'd sooner any damn thing! I'm going to tell her the whole truth immediately!

HUGO: Tell my aunt? Just take a look at who she's introducing to everybody, in the middle of the ballroom!

ROMAINVILLE: I'm too short-sighted. I can't see at this distance.

HUGO: Put your glasses on; it's worth it.

ROMAINVILLE [putting them on]: Good heavens! What on earth is she doing? Am I dreaming or is that . . .

HUGO: Yes. The Countess Funela. She used to revolve in the best Italian circles.

ROMAINVILLE: Is this you up to your tricks again?

HUGO: No. But my aunt is up to hers.

ROMAINVILLE: But why?

HUGO: No reason, which is what makes it serious.

PATRICE [entering aggressively]: Sir!

HUGO [who has entirely forgotten]: Sir?

PATRICE: This state of affairs cannot go on, and as you refuse to give the girl up – [He tries to box HUGO's ears.]

HUGO [pushing him tetchily away]: No, no, no! Another time! You're being a nuisance! Later on, later on! Come on, Romainville, we've got to go and stop her jumping in the lake.

[He goes, dragging ROMAINVILLE in a flurry after him.]

PATRICE: All right. I'll come back.

[He goes, jostled by the couples who fill the stage wildly dancing the polka.]

CURTAIN

ACT THREE

SCENE I

The same
ISABELLE *sits in the centre of the stage.* HUGO *walks about.*

ISABELLE: And so?

HUGO: And so it doesn't amuse me any more. And, anyway, that moronic mother of yours is going to drop every brick in the hod any moment now. Look at her: cooing and clucking and crowing, all our feathered friends rolled into one. She makes me shiver. She told General de Saint-Mouton that she's the Pope's god-daughter. He's delighted; he can see his Catholicism becoming profitable at last; he imagines he's Ambassador to the Vatican already!

ISABELLE: Am I still to throw myself into the lake?

HUGO: That's no good now; think of something better, and think quickly, or else my respectable undelectable aunt is quite likely to spoil the whole thing. I know! I've got it!

ISABELLE: You frighten me when you say that.

HUGO: There's no doubt you're still the attraction of the evening, in spite of your mother behaving like a circus. You've made a sensation: distinction, poise, reserve. Even the dowagers are on your side.

> What birdwings rocked her cradle, what swift grace
> > Caught her and taught her limbs to move
> Gravely as shadows in a sunlit place,
> > Or branches in a grove?

I walk behind you, gleaning the whispers, as flattered as if I were an impresario. Your effect on the men needs no comment. But all the mothers with marriageable daughters have shot their lorgnettes at you; and you emerge unscathed! You return triumphant from the underworld of undertones. And the daughters are white with fury. Where Diana fell they tumble after. But all this is only a

62

curtain-raiser, an appetizer, good enough to revive poor Frederic. Now I'm ready for better things! I'm going to start a rumour that you're not Romainville's niece at all, nor can your mother possibly be your mother. Better still, you're the wonderfully, wealthy side-issue of a Portuguese princess and an Admiral, an Admiral who wrote Byronic poetry and was drowned at sea (I shall think of one; there must have been several): and this is your coming-out party, incognito. And in the small hours, when my little puff ball of a story has been blown sufficiently from mouth to mouth, when my cuckoo-history has laid its eggs in the well-washed ears of all the little ladies, when Diana is withered with jealousy, when my abstracted brother, vaguely flattered by your smiling on him, has begun to look not quite so submissively at his executioner, I shall step from the wings, climb on a chair as though to announce the cotillion, crave silence and say to them more or less: 'My lords, ladies and gentlemen, you've been cuckooed!' And, making the most of the confusion, I shall continue: 'Dear asses! Tonight has been all a gullery; a fiction, all of it! Conceived, and planned, and carried out to the letter! During these few memorable hours you've been able to see [I shall say, calling on Diana to witness it] into the hearts of these young ladies: the rocks that lie there, the sediment, the dead flowers . . . And you have also been able to see [and my gesture will light on you] something too like an angel to be true! You've been made dupes of, ladies and gentlemen! What you have called distinction, breeding, poise, are only pretences. This angel, this girl who made your evening dazzle, is a lay-figure hired by me, a poor little ballet dancer from the Opéra brought here to play the part. She's not Romainville's niece, and she's not the daughter of any Byronic admiral: she is nothing at all. And no one would have more than barely noticed her if I'd brought her here to do her usual turn. But her turn tonight has been to represent yourselves. I've thrown her amongst you, dressed by your own dressmaker, using the words of your own kind, and this has been enough to knock sideways for a whole evening the prestige of your society beauty. "Vanity, vanity, all is vanity." I hope at least that my brother Frederic now sees the light. As for me, I find you unutterably dreary. I should be glad to have looked my last on the whole lot of you! Tomorrow I set off by the first train to hunt big game in Africa.' . . . How do you like that, Isabelle?

ISABELLE [*softly, after a pause*]: What happens to me?

HUGO: You! What do you mean?

ISABELLE: I mean, what becomes of me?

HUGO: What do you want to become of you? You go off home, with the present you well deserve, with your mother on your arm and you on Romainville's; and you have a nice dress and a happy memory. Nothing more than that ever remains of a night's dancing.

ISABELLE: You haven't thought I might be ashamed?

HUGO: Of what? You're a free spirit, and intelligent. You must loathe all these people as much as I do. Together we're going to have a good laugh at them. What better entertainment? You wouldn't want to be *like* them, would you?

ISABELLE: No, but . . . give the dress to someone else and let me go home! I'll call my mother; you can send us back to St Fleur *now*, and I promise no one will hear of me again.

HUGO: Nonsense!

ISABELLE: It may be, but . . . Not in front of your brother, then! Nor in front of you! Not just yet!

HUGO [*breaking free and going*]: Yes, now! This moment!

ISABELLE [*calling after him*]: It's wrong to think only of how it's going to amuse you!

HUGO: It's all there's time for, before we laugh on the other side of our graves.

[*He goes.*

ISABELLE *sinks on to the sofa again with a little hurt cry. Enter* DIANA. *She stands for a moment looking at* ISABELLE, *who raises her head and sees her.*]

DIANA: It's quite true; you're wearing a most attractive dress.

ISABELLE: Yes, it is.

DIANA: And you're looking beautiful; that's true, too.

ISABELLE: Thank you.

DIANA: Perhaps not perfectly groomed, still a little too close to nature and certainly not a very good powder, nor a very good perfume.

ISABELLE [*she has got up*]: That must be why I find yours a little too good, and you a little too far . . .

DIANA: Well? Too far what?

ISABELLE: From nature.

DIANA: You've managed quite well; but if one hasn't a maid who understands these things it's almost fatal; with the best will in the world one neglects oneself. No woman can tend herself and altogether survive. Do you get up early in the morning?

ISABELLE: Yes.

DIANA: Yes, one can see.

ISABELLE: Do you go late to bed?

DIANA: Yes.

ISABELLE: Yes, one can see.

DIANA: Thank you. Tell me, do you mind very much?

ISABELLE: Mind what?

DIANA: Wearing something you haven't made yourself?

ISABELLE: As a compensation, my eyelashes are my own.

DIANA: Happily for you. You'll need them tomorrow, without the help you get from the dress.

ISABELLE: I take it away with me. It was given me.

DIANA: That's very nice, isn't it? You'll be able to be a beauty all over again. I believe there's going to be a jolly dance on the fourteenth day of July at St Fleur. You'll turn all the bumpkins' heads. Do you like my dress?

ISABELLE: Yes, it's most beautiful.

DIANA: Would you like it? I shall never wear it again. I hardly ever wear a dress more than once. Besides, I can't really tell myself I like petunia. Tomorrow I shall dine in rose-pink, rather a miracle dress, a harass of little pleats, twenty yards of them. If you come up to my room I'll show it to you. Come and see it; I'm sure it'll give you pleasure.

ISABELLE: No.

DIANA: Why not? Do you envy me? That's one of the sins, you know. [*She goes to her.*] You'd love to be rich, wouldn't you? If this evening were only a true story, and you had as many dresses as I have!

ISABELLE: Naturally.

DIANA: But you'll never have more than one, isn't that so? And if I put my foot on your train, in this way, and tug it a little, you'll not even have one.

ISABELLE: Take your foot away!

DIANA: No.

ISABELLE: Take your foot away or else I shall hit you!

DIANA: Don't squirm, you little fury; you'll do some damage!
[*The dress tears.*]

ISABELLE [*with a sorrowful cry*]: Oh! My dress!

DIANA: You did it yourself. A few tacks, it will still do very nicely for St Fleur. It's exciting, I expect, to have such a triumphant evening with a borrowed dress on your back. The pity is, it's over so soon. Tomorrow morning you have to pack your cardboard box, and I shall still be here, and that's the difference between us.

ISABELLE [*looks at her without dislike, and suddenly says*]: Is it so pleasant to be unpleasant?

DIANA [*changing her tone, sitting and sighing*]: No, not at all. But one can't always be pleased.

ISABELLE: Can you be unhappy as well? That's very strange. Why?

DIANA: I have too much money.

ISABELLE: But Frederic loves you.

DIANA: I don't love him. I love Hugo, and he dislikes my money, and I think he's right.

ISABELLE: Become poor, then.

DIANA: Do you think it is so easy?

ISABELLE: I make no effort.

DIANA: You don't know how lucky you are. I suppose this is a lovely party – but all my friends give parties like it. I shall never again know the excitement of being 'invited up to the great house' – and that's so sad.

ISABELLE: So sad.

DIANA: I tell you, money is only worth something to the poor.

ISABELLE: Which proves there is something the matter with the world. [*She moves towards* DIANA.] I have been humiliated and hurt this evening, and my only dress has been torn, because I'm one of the poor ones. I'm going to do what the poor ones always do. I'm leaving words for deeds, and asking you to go away.

DIANA: Go away? Do you think you're in your own home, you little adventuress?

ISABELLE: Go and cry over your millions somewhere a long way off! I'm pretty stupid and very ashamed to have spent so many minutes trying to understand you. So now I shall use the arguments of the poor. If you don't go I shall throw you out.

DIANA: Throw me out? Let me see you try!

ISABELLE: You're going to see me try! And as you wouldn't care if I tore your dress, I shall tear your face instead: God has been unusually impartial, giving us one face each.

DIANA: You're a common little slut. Do you think I'm afraid?

ISABELLE: Not yet. But I think you may be.

[ISABELLE *leaps on* DIANA. *They fight.*]

DIANA: Oh! You'll ruin my hair!

ISABELLE: You have a maid to put it right! What does it matter?

DIANA [*fighting*]: I've got claws as well as you!

ISABELLE: Then use them!

[*They fight.* DIANA *suddenly stops and cries out*]:

DIANA: I was poor once, myself! When I was ten I fought all the little toughs on the docks at Istanbul!

[*They throw themselves at each other again and roll on the ground. Enter* JOSHUA, *who gives a yell of terror when he sees them and goes off shouting for* MR HUGO.

FREDERIC *enters immediately and stands speechless. The* GIRLS *see him and loose each other.* ISABELLE *rises first, scratched and dishevelled. She goes to him.*]

ISABELLE: Well, are you satisfied now! Don't you think you've had a great success? You wanted entertainment, and no one can now say you haven't had it. How is this for your scandal? You stood up on your chair and told them who I was: or if you haven't yet, you have no need to. I'm going to show myself to them, looking as I am. A common little slut, as this lady called me. You can watch your bit of fun get funnier. They'll have no doubts about me now; they'll know exactly where I come from! Do you want me to tell you the climax of the ball? To begin with, I insult my mother: I pluck her feathers in front of them all: and I take her away, back to her piano lessons. Down the wind goes the Countess Funela! Her father sold wallpaper; he carried the rolls on his back and a pastepot in his hand. They used to give him five francs a time, which kept him happy because it meant he could buy himself a drink without telling his wife. That's the poor for you! You wanted to play with them tonight because you were bored, but you'll see what a mistake it was, and how right your nurses were when you were little and they told you not to play with the common children in the park. They don't know how to play, and I haven't played for one moment since I came here. I've been unhappy: isn't that vulgar of me? I've been unhappy. And all because you didn't understand, or wouldn't understand, that I love you. It's because I love you that I've done my best to dazzle them this evening; it's because I love you that I've pretended to love your brother; it's because I love you that I was ready to throw myself in the lake, like a baby and a fool, to finish it all! If I hadn't loved you, and loved you from the moment we met, do you think I should have agreed to be in your mad puppet show? ... Well, won't you say something? It's tiresome, of course, this poor girl standing here saying she loves you. But please say *something*. You usually say so much. What's the matter?

FREDERIC [*stammering*]: But ... I'm afraid ... none of this was me.

ISABELLE: What do you mean, not me?

DIANA: Certainly it wasn't. Look at him. He's blushing: it's his brother!

ISABELLE [*suddenly confused*]: Oh, I'm so sorry ... I'm so very sorry.

FREDERIC: No, no, no. It's I who should be sorry. I should have ...

DIANA: Come away, Frederic. There's nothing you need say to this girl. Hugo will send Joshua along to pay her, and she can go home.

FREDERIC: Don't talk like that, Diana.

DIANA: You will come with me now, Frederic, at once, or from now on you can stay away from me.

  [*She goes.*]

FREDERIC: I came to tell you how distressed I am by what you've been made to go through this evening, how unpleasant and cruel I know it has been. May I ask you to accept my most sincere apologies for all the rest of them here?

ISABELLE [*gently*]: You must go. If you don't follow her quickly she's going to make you very wretched.

FREDERIC [*bowing*]: Will you excuse me, then? [*He takes a step.*] Shall I explain to my brother that you've told me you love him?

ISABELLE: No; there's no need.

  [FREDERIC *makes a sorrowful gesture – and goes.* THE MOTHER *sweeps in.*]

THE MOTHER: Oh, my dear child! Such mortification!

ISABELLE: I was coming to find you.

THE MOTHER [*sinking into a chair*]: Everything has collapsed! The young man has gone mad. He got up on to a chair, and said simply terrible things. There must be something really very wrong with his head. It's most unfortunate. If he had only waited for another hour I should have been spending the autumn with a General, a very nice one. But now everybody will turn their backs on me, I know they will.

ISABELLE [*rising*]: We're leaving now, Mother. Take off your finery. You have to give your piano lessons again next week.

THE MOTHER: You're quite extraordinary. There's not an ounce of poetry in you. All our brilliant dreams vanish, and you go on as usual. You're so insensitive. He couldn't have loved you, I suppose, and I was so convinced . . . Well, why, why should he have asked you here if he wasn't in love with you?

ISABELLE: You've talked quite enough. Go and take off your feathers.

THE MOTHER [*going to her*]: Now just listen to me. I've had a long conversation with Romainville. All this business this evening has nudged him awake, and he's spoken up at last. You've seen yourself this evening how the high-flown young men behave. Romainville is middle-aged, steady, and a gentleman. He has had his eye on you for a long time, he told me so himself: he knows just what he can expect. He isn't going into it with his eyes shut. So there you are. He'll see we're both taken good care of; moreover, he hasn't actually said, but I know he means, that when he has talked his family round he may even make a promise to marry you. Isn't that a nice surprise, dear?

ISABELLE: Now go upstairs.

THE MOTHER [*getting up, furious*]: All right then; go your own way; never think of me and all I've done for you! Lose a good chance, you stupid little ninny, and lose your looks, too, before they get you anywhere!

[MESSERSCHMANN *enters.*]

[*Suddenly all smiles*]: Oh, I'm so happy to see you! How do you do?

MESSER [*coldly*]: Well, madam.

THE MOTHER: The Countess Funela. We were introduced just now, but in such a hubbub . . .

MESSER: Madam, I must ask you to let me have a few moments alone with your daughter.

THE MOTHER: But of course you may. I give you my permission without any hesitation at all . . . I'm leaving you with Mr Messerschmann now, Isabelle. I'm going upstairs for a little rest. These social occasions, you know, are so tiring. One comes to wish for a little peace and quiet. We go out too much, I'm afraid, a great deal too much. I'll leave you . . . Don't forget about our good friend, Isabelle. We must give him an answer tonight, you know, to his charming invitation for the summer . . . Dear sir, I'm delighted to have seen you again!

[*She flounces away.*]

MESSER [*speaking straight out*]: Now, young lady, I'm going to be rather brutal. I know who you are, and in half an hour's time everybody will know. The party's over, as far as you're concerned. You've had a great success, everybody's been charmed by you, but it was a little adventure which couldn't last. I've come to ask you to cut it even shorter. Go up to your room and disappear without seeing anyone again. And I shall be most grateful to you.

ISABELLE: How can it affect you whether I go or stay?

MESSER: It's a little present I should like to give my daughter. You see, I make no bones about it. I've never deceived anyone in my business affairs, and I've always succeeded. How much do you want?

ISABELLE: Nothing. I had decided to go before you asked me.

MESSER: I know. But it isn't fair that you should go without being paid. How much did Hugo promise you?

ISABELLE: My usual dancing fee, and this dress, which someone has torn.

MESSER: Who tore it?

ISABELLE: Your daughter.

MESSER: Then that's my business, too. As well as what you were going to ask me, I'll pay for two more dresses.

ISABELLE: Thank you, but I'm happy with this one, with the tear.

MESSER: Let's get the situation clear. I don't want you to see Hugo again, even to get your fee. How much do I pay you to go without seeing him?

ISABELLE: Nothing at all. I didn't expect to see him.

MESSER: But how about the money he promised you?

ISABELLE: I don't intend to take it. I can be said to have danced here this evening for my own pleasure.

[MESSERSCHMANN *looks at her for a moment, in silence, then weightily and powerfully moves towards her.*]

MESSER: I don't like it when things don't cost anything, young lady.

ISABELLE: Does it disturb you?

MESSER: It's too expensive. Why are you refusing Hugo's money?

ISABELLE: Because I'm glad not to take it.

MESSER: And mine?

ISABELLE: Because you haven't any reason to give it to me. I was asked to act in a comedy here this evening. My performance is over, the curtain is down, and I'm going home.

MESSER: But not with nothing to show for it?

ISABELLE: Why not?

MESSER: It's not as it should be.

ISABELLE: I'm sorry, but it's what I'm going to do. You will excuse me. [*She starts to go.*]

MESSER [*suddenly furious*]: No, no, no! Don't be like Ossowitch!

ISABELLE [*stops, astonished*]: Like Ossowitch?

MESSER: Yes. He was a banker of a rival group, and I had to have important discussions with him. I never met such a man for getting up and going. Whenever we disagreed, which was pretty often, he got up and went. Every time I had to catch up with him in the vestibule or in the lift or somewhere. And the farther I had to go to catch him, the more it cost me. In the end I had to invite him to come out in a canoe, when I'd first made quite sure he couldn't swim. After that we were wonderfully good friends: but now he has learnt to swim and things are not so nice. So don't you start this getting up and going, my dear child, it isn't a good way to talk. Nobody ever agrees with anybody in a business discussion, but we stay sitting, or else business is no good. Now, come along, my dear young lady, be reasonable. Strike a good bargain with me before it's too late. What do you want?

ISABELLE: Nothing.

MESSER: It's too much. Now, look, I'm going to be foolish. I'm going to offer you twice what you expect. I've the notes on me here. [*He brings a bundle of notes from his pocket.*] Look at this bundle here, such virgins and so clean, such a pretty little bunch! It would be very nice, you will agree with me, to carry about a sprig or two of these little papers?

ISABELLE: How should I carry them?

MESSER [*suddenly like a shopkeeper*]: Would you like me to wrap them up for you? I could make you a nice little parcel of them.

ISABELLE: Listen. I don't want to have to walk out like Mr Ossowitch; I don't want to bring back unhappy memories to you; but I insist that you believe me. I don't want your money.

MESSER [*pocketing the notes, furious*]: You're being very exorbitant.

ISABELLE [*looks at him and says*]: Is it really possible to be a great power in the world without being very intelligent?

MESSER: I am intelligent! I'm very intelligent! It's because I'm very intelligent and experienced that I tell you I don't believe you!

ISABELLE [*taking him gently by the arm*]: Then, if you're intelligent, let's talk intelligently. If you hadn't kept me here I should have been gone already. So you see I have nothing to sell.

MESSER [*angrily*]: There's always something to sell! Anyway, even if you haven't, I've got to buy something now we've started bargaining.

ISABELLE: Why?

MESSER: Why? Because I should lose all faith in myself if I didn't.

ISABELLE [*with a slight smile*]: If it takes so little to make you lose faith, I must write to Mr Ossowitch.

MESSER [*calmer*]: Ossowitch was a baby. But you're an opponent who interests me. What I'm buying from you now isn't my daughter's peace of mind any more, it's my own peace of mind. And I put no limit whatsoever on that. How much do you want?

ISABELLE: Do men become masters of the world by continually repeating themselves?

MESSER: You're as rich as any girl in the house tonight. And if I want it, Romainville shall adopt you: you really will be his niece!

ISABELLE: Thank you.

MESSER: Listen. I'll make you so rich, the grandest and handsomest young fellow here will ask you to marry him immediately.

ISABELLE: I'm sorry. But none of that will please me as much as saying No to you.

MESSER [*suddenly howling*]: Whatever shall I do? I don't believe in money any more either! All it gives me is dust, smoke, nausea, and indigestion. I eat noodles and I drink water, and I get no pleasure at all from my frozen snow-queen mistress: I don't even suffer when she deceives me, because I don't really want her: I want nothing at all! I'm a poor little tailor from Cracow, and my only really pleasant memory is the first suit I made when I was sixteen: a jacket for a priest, and it turned out very well. My father said to me: 'This time you have done it well: you know now what your calling is.' And I was happy . . . but since then I've succeeded at nothing, except at making money, more and more money, and money has never made anybody love me, not even my own daughter. Please be sympathetic. Do stand by me this evening. Take my money!

ISABELLE: No.

MESSER: No? Ah well: now you can see what I'll do with these beautiful little bundles which can't do anything: I'll bite them and tear them with my teeth and spit them on the ground!

[*He has taken the bundle of notes and starts tearing them with his own teeth; then, soon, for the sake of speed, with his hands.*]

ISABELLE [*joyfully*]: What a good idea! Give me some, I'll help you. This will make me feel much better!

[*She takes some of the bundles and starts happily and quietly tearing them up. They throw the scraps of paper into the air. They both work feverishly in a rain of paper.*]

MESSER [*in a kind of fury*]: There! So! So! There! So! That's a country house: the dream of all the small householders!

ISABELLE [*tearing away merrily*]: With the garden, the pond, the gold-fish, the roses!

MESSER: Everything! There goes a business. A millinery business: the one I was going to give you, like the fool I was!

ISABELLE [*tearing*]: Hooray! That was a hat!

MESSER [*annoyed, but not stopping*]: Why only one hat?

ISABELLE: It was very expensive!

MESSER: There go the dresses, and still more dresses, rolls and folds and billows of material, what they're all dying to put on their backs. There go the cloaks and the coats and the wraps and the furs!

ISABELLE [*tearing*]: Not too many: it's nearly summer-time!

MESSER: Away goes the beautiful linen, the satin sheets, petticoats as light as cobwebs, embroidered handkerchiefs!

ISABELLE [*tearing*]: There goes a trunk!

MESSER [*stopping in surprise*]: Why a trunk?

ISABELLE: To put everything into!

MESSER [*starting again*]: There go the necklaces, the bracelets, the rings – all the rings!

ISABELLE [*tearing*]: Oh! Such a beautiful pearl!

MESSER: You'll regret that!

ISABELLE [*taking more to tear*]: No, not a bit!

MESSER: Away go the holidays abroad, the servants, the racehorses, the beautiful ladies ready and willing, away go the consciences of honest men, and all the prosperity of this lamentable world! There! There! There! There! [*He tears the last of the notes and turns to her.*] Are you happy now?

ISABELLE [*softly*]: No. Are you?

MESSER: Not at all.

[*They are kneeling side by side, exhausted.* ISABELLE *finds one untorn note on the ground and tears it up.*]

ISABELLE: There go the poor! We'd forgotten them. [*A pause. She looks at the exhausted* MESSERSCHMANN *and asks him gently*]: I bet it wasn't so exhausting to get it all?

MESSER: I'm very unhappy.

ISABELLE [*with a wry smile*]: Me, too.

MESSER: I understand very well how you feel. And I'm the only person in this house this evening who does understand. For a long time, such a long time, I was humiliated, until I became stronger than they were. Then I could turn the tables. Every man is quite alone. That's definite. No one can help anyone else: he can only go on.

[*They both look straight in front of them, squatting on the ground in the middle of the torn notes.* JOSHUA *enters and finds them so, to his surprise.*]

[*Seeing him*]: What do you want?

JOSHUA: It's Mr Hugo, sir: he wishes to speak to the young lady in the little drawing-room, to settle her account.

ISABELLE [*getting up*]: Tell him he doesn't owe me anything. Mr Messerschmann has paid me.

[*She goes.*]

[MESSERSCHMANN *watches her go, then rises with difficulty, with* JOSHUA'S *help.*]

MESSER: My friend.

JOSHUA: Sir?

MESSER: You seem to have a pleasant face.

JOSHUA [*after the first astonishment*]: I belong to a generation of old servants who could never permit themselves to have such a thing while on duty, sir. But on Sundays, and particularly on holidays, my friends tell me I have an amiable face, sir, almost jovial, what I hope I may call a nice face, very French and very homely, sir.

MESSER: Then listen to me. You must have read your Bible when you were a little boy?

JOSHUA: Here and there, sir, like everybody else.

MESSER: Did you ever come across Samson?

JOSHUA: The gentleman who had his hair cut, sir?

MESSER: Yes; and he was very unhappy. Jeered at, my friend, always jeered at by everybody. They had put his eyes out. They thought he was blind, but I'm sure he could see.

JOSHUA: Quite possible, sir . . .

MESSER: And then, one fine day, unable to stand it any more, he got them to lead him between the pillars of the temple. He was very strong, terribly strong, you understand? He twined his arms round the pillars . . . [*He puts his arms round the dismayed* JOSHUA.] Like this!

JOSHUA: Oh, sir! Do take care, sir, someone will see us!

MESSER: And then he shook them with all his might. [*He shakes* JOSHUA.]

JOSHUA [*being shaken*]: Yes, sir! Do be careful, sir! I'm the one who will get into trouble!

MESSER [*letting him go with a sigh, his feelings relieved*]: There!

JOSHUA [*putting himself to rights*]: Well, there, sir. [*He adds, for something to say*]: It wasn't at all the thing to do in a church . . .

MESSER [*with a dark chuckle*]: You might well say so. He was so strong the entire temple crumbled down on to the two thousand Philistines who were there praying to their false gods, and thinking Samson no better than a fool!

JOSHUA: But it fell on him, too, sir.

MESSER: It fell on him, too. But that wasn't of any kind of importance. How could being poor hurt him!

JOSHUA: If you say so, sir.

[*A pause.* JOSHUA *starts to go.*]

MESSER: My friend.

JOSHUA: Sir?

MESSER: I'm putting through an overseas telephone call from my room tonight.

JOSHUA: Certainly, sir.

MESSER: That's all. Like Samson. With my eyes tight shut.

JOSHUA [*going*]: Quite so, sir.

MESSER: And all at once there's a frightful uproar, a telephone ringing in the small hours. And that is the temple starting to crumble. Do you understand?

JOSHUA: No, sir.

MESSER: It doesn't matter. [*He finds a forgotten note in his pocket and gives it to* JOSHUA.] Here's a thousand francs. Forget everything I've said. [*As he goes out, he turns and says*]: And for supper, you remember . . . without butter.

JOSHUA [*bowing*]: And without salt.

CURTAIN

SCENE 2

As the lights begin to fade in, ISABELLE *is seen wandering across the stage. She drifts across the bridge and away into the park towards the lake.*

MADAME DESMERMORTES *wheels herself in, watching* ISABELLE *through her opera glasses.*

CAPULAT *enters in a terrible state.*

CAPULAT: Madam, madam! Everyone's searching the place for Isabelle. Her mother is out of her mind!

MME DESMER: Why?

CAPULAT: She has left her ring, the only valuable thing she has, wrapped up in a piece of paper on her dressing-table. Oh, madam, madam, we're all to blame! Mr Hugo didn't love her!

MME DESMER: You can cry later on, Capulat. Look out there, down to the lake; I can't see. Is there a white figure there?

CAPULAT: There is, you're quite right. And it's Isabelle, it really is, it is really! Oh dear, oh dear, unhappy girl! Oh, madam, she's leaning over the water. Oh, madam, madam, madam, she has jumped! Rescue her! Rescue her! She'll be drowned, really she will, she will really!

MME DESMER: No, she won't. Hugo is down there, and there isn't enough water. But she might quite well catch cold, and so might he. Run and get some blankets.

CAPULAT: Mr Hugo is there, you're quite right, he's there. He has plunged into the water – oh, hero! It's all right, I think, madam, it's all right. He'll save her.

MME DESMER: It could hardly be less difficult.

CAPULAT: He has picked her up in his arms, he has really, and they're coming glittering across the grass in an armour of moisture, madam, as you might say.

MME DESMER: As I certainly wouldn't say. Stop talking nonsense, you stupid woman, and go at once and find some blankets.

[CAPULAT *hurries off.*]

Joshua! Joshua! Someone! Quickly!

JOSHUA [*appearing*]: Madam?

MME DESMER: I'm afraid we're having a little drama here this evening, Joshua: heartbreak and attempted death by water. I'm so sorry. Do go down to the kitchens and make some very hot punch.

JOSHUA: Yes, madam. Nothing serious, I hope?

MME DESMER: Not at all. What a blessing you are, Joshua. Do try never to break *your* heart, won't you?

JOSHUA: I handle it with as much care, madam, as if it was yours. It's quite safe with me, madam.

MME DESMER: The punch, Joshua.

JOSHUA [*bowing*]: Hot and very soon, madam.

[*As he goes – enter* HUGO *and* ISABELLE *wrapped in blankets, and followed by* CAPULAT.]

CAPULAT: They're safe, madam, they're safe, but they're wet!

MME DESMER: I can show almost no surprise. Go and tell your friend that her daughter is well.

CAPULAT: I will. She was out of her mind!

[*She goes.*]

MME DESMER: Are you cold, my dear?

ISABELLE: No, thanks; no, no, I'm not.

MME DESMER: Joshua has gone to fetch you some punch. Are you cold, Hugo?

HUGO: Frozen, thank you, aunt.

MME DESMER: Then let's make the most of being alone for a few minutes. Stay as you are. Sit down. Sit down, Hugo. Now, look at me, my dear.

[ISABELLE *looks at her.*]

She looks even prettier with her hair down. Why do you ever wear it up?

ISABELLE: It's the usual way.

MME DESMER: Is it also the usual way, at the first crossing of love, to walk into a lake? You can swim, I imagine?

ISABELLE: Yes, I can swim.

MME DESMER: You see how absurd you are!

HUGO: I suppose it was my fault. I asked her to pretend to drown herself for love of Frederic; but I cancelled the arrangement immediately afterwards. I simply don't know what she thought she was doing.

MME DESMER: Why should you want to drown yourself?

ISABELLE: For my own reasons.

HUGO: It wasn't in our agreement. You were supposed to do what you were told.

ISABELLE: My working-day was over. You had already sent the butler to pay me; and I think I'm allowed to kill myself in my own free time, if I want to.

MME DESMER: Certainly she is! And it's very nearly morning, and Sunday morning, too. If a working-man can't kill himself on a Sunday morning we can have the revolution at once.

> For pity, pretty eyes, surcease
> To give me war! and grant me peace.

You know you're a madman, don't you, Hugo?

HUGO: Yes, Aunt.

MME DESMER: He doesn't love you, my dear, and he'll never love you. He'll never love anyone, I think, if that's any consolation to you. He'll be amorous, perhaps, like a cat with a mouse, from time to time; but you're too delicate a mouse: he would eat you too soon, which he wouldn't like at all. And I'm going to tell you a splendid thing: he's not your sort of cat, either. You think you're in love with him. In fact, you're not in love with him at all. Look at him. Look at him. Look at this sulky Red Indian. Isn't he comic?

[ISABELLE *looks at* HUGO.]

You find him so handsome? Well, so he is, tolerably, when he's not thinking of anything. Clear eyes, straight nose, an interesting mouth. But let even the smallest of his wicked little thoughts creep into him – look at him now, for instance: we're irritating him: he wants to strangle us – and the change is quite terrifying. The nose is getting pinched, there's an angry little crease tugging the mouth, the eyes are turning themselves into gimlets . . . And this chin! It suddenly makes him, wouldn't you say, into a fairly pretty but entirely wicked old woman? No one's altogether handsome who isn't altogether human.

HUGO [*getting up in a rage*]: That's quite enough! If you want to analyse faces I'll go and send Frederic to you.

MME DESMER: That's a very good idea.

[HUGO *goes.*]

No, my dear, it's the appearance of Hugo you love, not Hugo.

ISABELLE [*hiding her eyes and crying*]: Oh, it's terrible!

MME DESMER: It would be terrible, if we only had one specimen; but fortunately we have two.

[FREDERIC *enters.*]

[*To* FREDERIC] Come here, my nephew. You can look at him, Isabelle; it's the same picture as before. Here is a young woman who was going to drown herself, and we can't get her to tell us why.

FREDERIC [*to* ISABELLE]: I know why. I wish I could help you, but there's nothing I can do. There's something I want to tell you. When I left you just now I was being a coward for the last time. I followed Diana when she told me to. But when I caught her up I couldn't help telling her how wickedly she had treated you. And it's all over now: our engagement is broken off.

ISABELLE: Oh, no, no! Do you think it does any good for us both to be unhappy at once?

FREDERIC: I don't know, but I do know I couldn't love someone who could be so cruel.

MME DESMER: Neither can Isabelle. She's beginning to see she could never love Hugo.

FREDERIC: I've finished with love altogether. I saw down to the sea-bed of a woman's heart.

ISABELLE [*smiling gently*]: The rocks that lie there, the sediment, the dead flowers, as your brother said.

FREDERIC: It's the worst plunge I ever took.

MME DESMER: Come up to the surface again; there's still some dry land in places.

FREDERIC: I'm going to find a desert island, out of the way of it all.

MME DESMER: And so is Isabelle. Make sure that your desert islands aren't too far apart. You can have visiting days, hermit to hermit.

FREDERIC: I could have forgiven her for being unkind . . .

ISABELLE: I saw from the first I had to take him as he was, and forgave him for that, but . . .

FREDERIC: I could have forgiven her for being hard, egotistical, and hot-tempered . . .

ISABELLE: I could have forgiven him . . .

MME DESMER: The only thing you could never forgive them was not loving you. We're terrible tailors! We cut the cloth, take no measurements, and when it doesn't fit we cry for help.

FREDERIC: And no one comes.

MME DESMER: Or so we think. Not content with being blind we have to be deaf as well. We all go howling along together, never seeing or hearing who's beside us, and then we say we're in a wilderness! Luckily there are certain old women who have begun to see more clearly, just at the time, alas, when they're having to take to spectacles. Didn't you hear anything, young lady? This young gentleman called for help.

ISABELLE: How can I help him?

MME DESMER: You can take him into the park and tell him why you feel so unhappy. And he'll tell you why his life seems over. Go along; be as sad as you possibly can; give her your arm, Frederic. You're quite alone in the world. No one is more hopeless than you are.

FREDERIC [*going with* ISABELLE]: It's my own fault for being such a fool. I imagined women could be warm-hearted and have sincerity.

ISABELLE: And, of course, they can't. I imagined men could be honest and good and faithful.

FREDERIC: Faithful! We're faithful to ourselves, that's all. We dance the dance of the heart obstinately in front of a mirror. But I expected the dance to be with a partner.

ISABELLE: And there are no partners . . .

[*They have gone.* MME DESMERMORTES *watches them off.*]

MME DESMER: Good. Those two only need another five minutes. Now for the others. [*She calls.*] Hugo!

[HUGO *enters by another door.*]

HUGO: Yes, Aunt?

MME DESMER: That's as good as done. Now what have you decided?

HUGO: What do you want me to decide?

MME DESMER: Either I'm a dense and myopic old woman, my dearest Hugo, or you're in love with Diana, and she with you, and you have been since the first day you met.

HUGO: Absolutely ludicrous! And even if it were true, I'd rather die of jaundice, like your friend Palestrini you were talking about, than give her the pleasure of hearing me say so.

MME DESMER: You can't die of jaundice – Palestrini's as well as you or I. Only last year he threw himself into a lagoon because he was in love with an Austrian swimming champion. She rescued him, and they have a baby.

[*Enter* PATRICE BOMBELLES.]

PATRICE: Oh, there you are, I've been looking for you everywhere.

MME DESMER: What does this madman want?

PATRICE: Sir, as you will not give this young woman up of your own accord . . . [*He slaps* HUGO'S *face.*]

HUGO [*slapping back*]: Go away, for heaven's sake. I won't have you making such a confounded nuisance of yourself.

PATRICE: Well, may you be forgiven . . .

HUGO: May I be forgiven . . . Are you insulting me?

PATRICE: Yes, I am insulting you. You told me to insult you.

HUGO: Well, now I'm telling you to stop insulting me. Go away for goodness' sake . . .

PATRICE: I demand satisfaction . . .

HUGO: If you don't go I shall knock you down.

PATRICE: The arrangement was pistols – the arrangement was pistols.

[HUGO *leaps on* PATRICE. *They fight in spite of* MME DESMER-
MORTES *trying to separate them with her stick. Enter* LADY INDIA,
terrified.]

LADY INDIA: Patrice!

PATRICE [*freeing himself at once*]: Oh, my goodness, look, she's here!
Do try to seem friendly. [*He puts his arm round* HUGO'S *shoulder.*]
We were playing, my dear! We love playing together! A little
early morning exercise, you know.

LADY INDIA: This is no time to be taking exercise, Patrice! Do you
know what has happened? I've had a call from Paris. Messerschmann is out of his mind. He is selling in London, he is selling in
New York, he is selling in Paris. He's ruining himself!

PATRICE: I don't believe it. I'll go and ring up his agent!

[*He rushes out.* DIANA *enters.*]

DIANA: Have you heard the news? Within six hours my father will
be a poor man.

HUGO: What are you going to do about it!

DIANA: Be poor. What do you expect me to do?

HUGO: Marry Frederic, who is rich.

DIANA: I don't want him. And now he doesn't want me. Look at
him, down there in the park with the little adventuress. She hasn't
lost much time tonight. Was it you, Hugo, who taught her how to
find a rich husband in one evening? You will have to teach me. I
need one now.

HUGO: Let's be quite clear about this: it's a lesson that wouldn't help
you in the least.

[*He starts to go.* MME DESMERMORTES *stops him.*]

MME DESMER: Hugo, where are you going?

HUGO: I'm going to find Frederic. It's no good his thinking he can
break the engagement now. Diana's ruined, and the honourable
thing is to make her his wife.

DIANA [*in tears*]: But I don't want him!

HUGO: We can't help that.

[*He goes.*]

MME DESMER: *Mille tonnerres!* He's going to mix everything up
again!

[*Enter* CAPULAT *and* THE MOTHER.]

CAPULAT: Madam! News! Extraordinary news! It really is!

MME DESMER: I think we have heard it.

THE MOTHER: You've heard it? Now how could that possibly be? But news travels so fast these days. Here he is, to tell you himself. [*Wedding March from the orchestra. Enter* ROMAINVILLE *in morning coat and white gloves, carrying a bouquet. He goes to* MME DESMER-MORTES.]

ROMAINVILLE: My dear friend. In the first place, please excuse my clothes, but as dawn is about to break I changed into a morning coat: I felt it to be the correct wear for the present occasion. I'm going to give you some interesting news: my niece, dear friend, is not my niece – that was an entirely imaginary relationship spun from your nephew's fancy. But she is about to become even more nearly related. After extremely careful thought, I've decided to marry her.

MME DESMER: My good man, I would be the first to congratulate you, but I have an idea that you're too late.

ROMAINVILLE: Too late? What can you mean? It's five o'clock in the morning.

[ISABELLE *and* FREDERIC *come in with their arms round one another.*]

MME DESMER [*to* ISABELLE *and* FREDERIC]: Well, my dears, what news have you for us? Have you altered the fit of the coat?

ISABELLE: There wasn't any need to alter it! It fitted perfectly!

FREDERIC: Aunt, I must have been out of my mind. I don't love you any more, Diana; do forgive me.

ISABELLE: Why couldn't I have known it before! It was Frederic, just as you said.

MME DESMER: Romainville, you'll have to get some other niece. This is the one you have to give away!

ROMAINVILLE: It's appalling! I had just begun to like the idea!

[JOSHUA *enters, carrying a tray.*]

MME DESMER [*to* JOSHUA]: Joshua, give him some of the punch. [ROMAINVILLE *drinks the punch.*] But where is Hugo! Someone go and find him at once. He has made this girl unhappy for quite long enough. [*To* DIANA.] Don't be too dismayed; he loves you, he told me so.

LADY INDIA: Why, look! He's down there in the park, escaping!

MME DESMER: Escaping? Joshua, catch him before he goes, and bring him here.

[JOSHUA *goes.*]

[*To* DIANA.] He's a thoroughly crack-brained boy, but he knows he's cornered; he's certain to come back.

DIANA: But suppose he doesn't love me?

MME DESMER: Impossible. Everything has to end happily, it's only decent. Besides, here he is. Well, Hugo?

[*They all look at the door through which* HUGO *should come. A pause. It is* JOSHUA *who enters.*]

FREDERIC: I knew he wouldn't come!

JOSHUA: Mr Hugo has given me this note for you, madam.

MME DESMER: Read it aloud, Joshua.

JOSHUA [*puts on his glasses and reads*]: 'Dear Aunt, For reasons which you all know, I'm not able to appear among you to take part in the general rejoicing. There's nothing I've ever regretted more. But now Diana is poor I know I love her. Nothing will separate us again. I shall marry her. Tell her to look for me in the park.'

MME DESMER [*to the happy* DIANA]: Off you go!

DIANA: Yes, I will! Oh, Hugo! Hugo!

[DIANA *goes*.

Enter MESSERSCHMANN *with a little overcoat, a little hat, a little suitcase. Mocking music from the orchestra.*]

MME DESMER: What's this, will someone tell me?

MESSER: It is I, madam. I've come to say good-bye.

MME DESMER: But the suitcase, the hat, the coat?

MESSER: I borrowed them from your butler. I've nothing of my own to put on. I'm ruined. I shall return them in a few years' time. I'm going back to Cracow, on foot, to start a small tailoring business.

LADY INDIA [*running into his arms*]: Oh, my darling boy, what a great, great man you are after all! You must love me so much, so beautifully. It was for me, wasn't it, that you ruined yourself? I'll follow you: barefooted to the bottom of the Steppes of Siberia!

MME DESMER [*to the others*]: She gets so muddled.

LADY INDIA: I'll cook for you, my darling, in your dark, dingy igloo, ever your faithful squaw.

MME DESMER: She hasn't even a working idea of geography.

[*A frightful racket suddenly, flashes and bangs. Everybody turns round. Enter* PATRICE BOMBELLES.]

PATRICE: There they go! They've started!

LADY INDIA: What is it? The fire from heaven already?

MME DESMER: No. We haven't deserved that, not quite, not yet. It's my firework display, which all the upset tonight has made a little late. Come along, come and watch: the gardener will be so disappointed if we don't. It will feel rather odd, in broad daylight. We shall hardly be able to see them.

[*As they all go out – enter* JOSHUA *with a telegram. He plucks* MESSERSCHMANN *by the sleeve.*]

JOSHUA: Sir, a telegram for you, sir.

MESSER [*opening it*]: Who is still sufficiently interested in me to send me a telegram? A letter would have done just as well. [*He reads it and sighs.*] How funny it all is . . .

JOSHUA [*compassionately*]: All over, sir, is it? If you should still need anything, sir . . . I've got a small amount in the savings-bank . . .

MESSER: What? No, thank you. It's not so easy to ruin yourself as you'd think. It was believed to be a manoeuvre on the stock exchange. They bought everything, and now I'm twice as rich as I was before! . . . But I do beg of you: don't let anyone know.

JOSHUA: I must say, I'm very happy for you, sir. I should have felt very sad, sir, not to have brought you your breakfast. [*He has taken up his butler's stance, and says*]: Without butter?

MESSER: Yes, my friend. But this morning, as a special celebration, you may add a little salt.

JOSHUA [*following him*]: Ah, it's a happy day for me, sir, to see you taking such a pleasure in life again . . .

[*They go.*]

CURTAIN

UGO BETTI

The Queen and the Rebels

La regina e gli insorti

TRANSLATED BY
HENRY REED

THE QUEEN AND THE REBELS

The Queen and the Rebels was performed at the Haymarket
Theatre, London, on 26 October 1955, with the following
cast:

ARGIA	Irene Worth
ELISABETTA	Gwendoline Watford
AMOS	Leo McKern
BIANTE	Alan Tilvern
RAIM	Duncan Lamont
THE PORTER	John Kidd
MAUPA	Brian Wallace
AN ENGINEER	John Gill
A PEASANT	Patrick Magee
A PEASANT-WOMAN	Mary Llewellin
A YOUNG PEASANT	Angela Lloyd

Travellers, Peasants, Soldiers: John Herrington, John Nettleton, Gordon Richardson, Jack Good, John Ronane, Kevin O'Keeffe, Kenneth Toye, Joe Goodman, Patricia Kneale

The time is the present day

The Play was produced by Frank Hauser
The Scenery was designed by Audrey Cruddas
The Play was presented by Henry Sherek

ACT ONE

The scene, which is the same throughout the play, represents a large hall in the main public building in a hill-side village. There are signs of disorder and neglect.

The stage is empty when the curtain rises. The time is sunset. After a moment the HALL-PORTER *comes in. He is humble and apologetic in manner.*

THE PORTER [*to someone behind him*]: Will you come this way, please?
    [*A group of men and women come silently into the room. They are all carrying travelling-bags and cases.*]

THE PORTER: You can all wait in here for the time being.

ONE OF THE TRAVELLERS [*cautiously*]: We could wait just as well outside.

THE PORTER: Yes, but you can sit down in here. You'll find everything you want. This used to be the town-hall.

THE TRAVELLER: But we don't want to sit down. We want to get on. We're several hours late as it is.

THE PORTER: I'm sorry, sir. But you'll be all right in here. There are plenty of rooms, even if you have to stay the night.

THE TRAVELLER: Well, let's hope we don't have to stay the night! They told us we'd only be here half an hour, while the engine was cooling down.

THE PORTER: Yes, it's a stiff climb up here. The roads up those hills are very steep.

THE TRAVELLER: This is the third time they've stopped us to look at our papers. [*After a pause.*] I'm a district engineer. I . . . [*dropping his voice*] Do you think they've some special reason for stopping us?

THE PORTER: No, no. They'll let you go on directly.

THE ENGINEER: Yes, but what are we waiting for?

THE PORTER: Sir, I . . . I really don't know what to say. I'm only the hall-porter here. That's to say, I *was* the hall-porter. Since the trouble began, I've been alone here. I have to look after everything. Anyway, will you all make yourselves comfortable?

THE ENGINEER: Is it possible to telegraph from here? Or telephone?

THE PORTER: All the lines are down. We're cut off from the world. And we're very out of the way here, in any case. I'll go and see if I can find you some blankets. [*A pause.*]

THE ENGINEER: Look here: I can only speak for myself, of course, but I dare say these other ladies and gentlemen feel much the same as I do about this. You surely realize that nobody's going to travel about just now unless they have to. Every one of us here has some important business or other to attend to. We've all been given permits to travel. Otherwise we wouldn't have come up here at a time like this. We aren't political people; we're just ordinary peaceful travellers. We've all had to pay very large sums of money for a wretched little seat in that lorry out there. And we've all had to get permission from –

THE PORTER [*clearly unconvinced by his own words*]: But you'll see, sir: they'll let you go on directly. [*A pause.*]

THE ENGINEER: Do you know who's in charge here?

THE PORTER: *I* don't, no, sir. I just take orders from everybody else.

THE ENGINEER: Is there anybody we can speak to?

THE PORTER: The trouble is they keep coming and going the whole time. They say there's a general expected here this evening; and a commissar.

THE ENGINEER: Then there's no one here now that we can speak to?

THE PORTER: The N.C.O.s are a bit rough-spoken, sir. The only one would be the interpreter. But no one takes much notice of him either, I'm afraid.

THE ENGINEER: Interpreter? What do they need an interpreter for?

THE PORTER: Oh, he's just an interpreter. He's an educated young man.

THE ENGINEER: Very well, then: fetch the interpreter.

THE PORTER: I'll get him, sir.

[*He goes out. The travellers sit down silently, here and there.*]

THE ENGINEER: I don't suppose it's anything to worry about. I saw some other people outside. They'd been held up too. It's obviously only another examination because we're so near the frontier. My own papers are all in order. But if there *is* anyone here who's . . . travelling irregularly . . . it might perhaps be as well if they had the courage to speak up straight away, and say so; before they get us all into trouble.

ANOTHER TRAVELLER [*as though speaking to himself*]: The large number of spies about the place doesn't exactly inspire people with much desire to 'speak up', as you call it. In any case, it's obvious no one here is travelling irregularly. That would have been a little too simple-minded; or so I should have thought.

THE ENGINEER: Well, if that's the case, we ought to be on our way again in half an hour or so.

THE TRAVELLER: I can't say I share your optimism. It's been rather an odd journey, all along. Why did they make us come round this way in the first place? This village wasn't on our route at all. And the engine didn't need to cool down either. And why do we have all these inspections, anyway? The only reasonable explanation is that they're looking for someone.

THE ENGINEER: One of us?

THE TRAVELLER: Though it's just as likely that they're simply being stupid and awkward, as usual. That's about all nine-tenths of the revolution comes to.

THE ENGINEER: I . . . think we'd better change the subject, if you don't mind. There's no point in . . .

THE TRAVELLER: In what?

THE ENGINEER: Well, after all, this upheaval has very great possibilities, when all's said and done.

THE TRAVELLER: You really think so?

THE ENGINEER: Yes. Yes, I do. Quite sincerely.

THE TRAVELLER: Couldn't you . . . spare yourself this extreme cautiousness? It looks rather as if the extremists aren't doing too well at the moment. You didn't notice, as we came along the road?

THE ENGINEER: Notice what?

THE TRAVELLER: Over towards the mountains. That faint crackling sound every now and then.

THE ENGINEER: What was it?

THE TRAVELLER: Rifle-fire. They're fighting near here, on the far slope. Everything's hanging by a thread at the moment. It's possible the Unitary Government won't last the week out.

THE ENGINEER: A week. It doesn't take a week to shoot anybody. [*He drops his voice.*] I didn't notice the noises; I was too busy noticing the smell. Did you . . . catch that smell every now and then?

THE TRAVELLER: It's the smell of history.

THE ENGINEER: They don't even take the trouble to bury them.

[*The* PORTER *comes in.* RAIM, *the interpreter, follows him, blustering and bombastic. He pretends not to deign to glance at the group of travellers.*]

THE PORTER [*as he enters*]: The interpreter's just coming.

RAIM [*off*]: Where are they? Foreign slaves and spies, that's what they'll be. [*Entering.*] Where are the reactionary traitors?

THE ENGINEER [*amiably*]: You can see that we are not reactionaries. We are nothing of the kind.

RAIM: Then you must be filthy loyalists; a lot of monarchist swine.

THE ENGINEER: I assure you you're mistaken.

RAIM: You're enemies of the people. What have you come up here for? We fight and die, up here! Have you come up here to spy on us? Are you trying to smuggle currency across the frontier?

THE ENGINEER: We are ordinary peaceful travellers. Our papers have been inspected and stamped over and over again. I must ask you once again to rest assured that we are all sympathizers with the League of Councils.

RAIM [*satirically*]: Oh, yes, I knew you'd say that. You're a lot of exploiters, all of you. [*He drops his voice a little.*] And stuffed to the neck with money, I'll bet.

THE ENGINEER: No, sir.

RAIM: Poor little things. No money. We shall see about that.

THE ENGINEER: Not one of us has any money above the permitted amount.

RAIM: Gold, then? Valuables.

THE ENGINEER: No, sir. We all have permission to travel. We merely wish to be allowed to proceed on our way. On the lorry.

RAIM: I'm afraid you'll find that lorry's been requisitioned.

[*A silence.*]

THE ENGINEER: Shall we . . . be able to go on . . . by any other means?

RAIM: The road's blocked. In any case the bridges have all been blown up.

[*A silence.*]

THE ENGINEER: In that case, will you allow us to go back again to our families?

RAIM: Oh, yes, *I'm* sure! You people, you come up here, and poke your noses into everything, and then go back home and tell tales. I've a pretty shrewd suspicion you'll have to wait here.

THE TRAVELLER: And what shall we be waiting for?

RAIM: The requisite inspections.

THE TRAVELLER: Has anyone authorized you to speak in this way?

RAIM: Has anyone authorized you to poke your nose in?

THE TRAVELLER: On what precise powers do you base your right to interfere with our movements?

RAIM: My powers are my duties as a good citizen of the republic. I act for the republic. And you? What are you waiting for? Show me your hands. Come on.

[*The* TRAVELLER *holds out his hands.*]

RAIM: Proper priest's hands, aren't they just? *You've* never worked for your living. A bishop at least, I should say.

THE TRAVELLER: Your own hands seem to be very well kept ones too.

RAIM: Thanks, your reverence, very clever, aren't you? Yes: a great pianist's hands, mine are. A pity I can't play. [*He laughs, and turns to the* PORTER.] Orazio, collect these people's documents.

[*The* PORTER *begins to collect the documents.*]

THE TRAVELLER: Will *you* be examining them?

RAIM: They'll be inspected by Commissar Amos. We're expecting him any minute. Or better still, General Biante. He'll be here as well, very soon. Yes! Amos and Biante! Are those gigantic figures big enough for you?

THE TRAVELLER: Quite.

RAIM: In the meanwhile, let me hear you say very clearly the word: purchase.

THE TRAVELLER: Purchase.

RAIM: Centre.

THE TRAVELLER: Centre.

RAIM: Now say: January.

THE TRAVELLER: January.

RAIM: Can't say I like your accent very much. You wouldn't be a dirty refugee, by any chance?

THE TRAVELLER: Your own accent isn't particularly good either, if I may say so.

RAIM: Ah, but I'm the interpreter, your reverence. I'm unfortunately obliged to soil my lips with foreign expressions. See? Give me this man's papers, Orazio. [*After a pause.*] You claim to have been born in the High Redon, I see.

THE TRAVELLER: Yes.

RAIM: Are you a Slav?

THE TRAVELLER: No.

RAIM: Your surname looks like an alien's to me. Are you a Catholic?

THE TRAVELLER: No.

RAIM: Orthodox? Protestant? Jew?

THE TRAVELLER: I haven't decided yet.

RAIM: Good: but I shouldn't take too long about it. Do you live on investments?

THE TRAVELLER: No.

RAIM: Do you own large estates?

THE TRAVELLER: No.

RAIM: Gold?

THE TRAVELLER: No.

RAIM: Bonds?

THE TRAVELLER: No.

RAIM: What are your political opinions?

THE TRAVELLER: I cannot deny that I feel a certain concern for the Queen.

[*A silence. Everyone has turned to look at him.*]

RAIM: The Queen?

THE TRAVELLER: The Queen.

RAIM: Good. We'll see how you like trying to be funny when Biante and Amos get here. [*Rudely, to another of the travellers.*] You. Show me your hands. [*To another.*] You.

[*The person in front of him is a timid, shabbily-dressed peasant-woman. She puts out her hands, at which he glances in disgust.*]

RAIM: Peasant. [*Turning to the* PORTER.] Even peasants can travel all over the place, these days! [*Turning back to the travellers, with his finger pointing.*] You.

[*He stands there speechless, with his finger still pointing. He is facing a rather attractive woman, with crumpled but not unpretentious clothes,*] *and badly dyed hair. She has hitherto remained hidden among the other travellers. She stares at him: and slowly puts out her hands.*]

ARGIE [*in quiet tones, half-teasing and half-defiant*] : I have never done a stroke of work in my life. I have always had a very large number of servants at my disposal.

[*They have all turned to look at her.* RAIM *stands there embarrassed, and seeking some way out of his embarrassment. He turns abruptly to the* TRAVELLER.]

RAIM : You, sir : *You*, I mean!

THE TRAVELLER [*politely*] : Yes? Is there something else I can . . .?

RAIM : I've been thinking : I didn't like the way you . . . your manner of . . .

THE TRAVELLER : Yes?

RAIM [*still trying to recover his self-possession*] : I'm afraid this . . . this casual manner of yours demands closer attention. And the rest of you too : I shall have to go into things in more detail. We must get these things straight. Orazio, you'll bring these people into my room . . . in small groups . . . or better perhaps, one by one, separately. Yes. These things have to be dealt with quietly, calmly. [*He has gone over to the door. Turning back.*] I'd like you all to understand me. You mustn't think I'm doing all this out of spite. On the contrary, you'll find I'm really a friend. It's a devil's cauldron up here : everything in a state of confusion. All sorts of different people . . . different races and languages, infiltrators, priests with beards, priests without; everything you can think of : this spot here's a picture of the whole world in its small way. There's too much friction everywhere. Why shouldn't we all try to help one another? Rich and poor, poor and rich. What I mean is, I should be very happy if I could . . . assist any of you. Orazio, send them all in to me. [*He goes out.*]

THE PORTER [*after a very brief pause*] : Well, come on. You first . . . and you.

[*He points first to one, then to another of the travellers. They follow* RAIM.]

THE ENGINEER : Well, it's just as I said : another inspection.

THE PORTER [*with a quick glance at* ARGIA] : Yes. They've been tightening things up since this morning.

ARGIA [*lighting a cigarette*] : But are they really looking for somebody?

THE PORTER: Well . . . there's a lot of gossip flying about. [*He casts another furtive glance at her.*]

ARGIA: Is it . . . the so-called 'Queen' they're after?

THE PORTER [*evasively*]: That's what people are saying.

THE ENGINEER: My dear fellows, all this talk about the woman they call the Queen, just goes to show what a ridiculous race of people we are.

ARGIA [*smoking*]: I thought the clever lady died, five years ago?

THE TRAVELLER [*intervening*]: Yes, so it's said. But the ordinary people still maintain that in the cellar at Bielovice the body of the woman was never found.

THE PORTER: They were all of them in that cellar to begin with: when they were alive: ministers, generals, and so on.

ARGIA: And was she there too?

THE TRAVELLER [*to* ARGIA *with detachment*]: Yes, she was. Haven't you ever heard about it? It's quite a story. It's claimed that when the soldiers poured their machine-gun fire down through the barred windows, they instinctively omitted to aim at the woman. So that after the job was finished, under all those bloody corpses . . .

THE ENGINEER [*sarcastically*]: . . . the cause of all the trouble was unharmed.

THE TRAVELLER [*to* ARGIA, *as before*]: There were four soldiers on guard at the Nistria bridge, up in the mountains. In the evening a woman appeared. She was covered in blood from head to foot. The soldiers said: 'Where are you going?' She looked at them, and said: 'Are you sure you have any right to ask me that?' The soldiers said they had orders to stop everyone, especially women. She said: 'Are you looking for the Queen?' 'Yes,' they said. She looked at them again, and said: 'I am the Queen. What are my crimes?'

ARGIA: She wasn't lacking in courage.

THE TRAVELLER: No. She spoke with such calmness, and went on her way with such dignity that the soldiers didn't recover till the woman had disappeared into the woods.

THE ENGINEER: Very moving. And from then on, according to you, in a country like this, with more traitors than there are leaves on the trees, that woman has been able to stay in hiding for five years?

THE TRAVELLER: Very few people actually knew her. She always remained in the background.

THE ENGINEER [*ironically*]: It's a pretty little tale. In any case what reasons would such a woman have now for springing up out of the ground? Events have passed her by. All the parties either hate her or have forgotten her, which is worse. And why do you call her the Queen? She was never that. Even her most slavish accomplices never flattered her to that extent.

THE TRAVELLER [*gently*]: All the same, the common people have taken to calling her by that name.

THE ENGINEER: The common people have always been fascinated by the major gangsters. Especially blue-blooded ones. That great lady was not only the blazoned aristocratic wife of a usurper; she was the real usurper and intriguer herself. She was the evil genius behind everything, the Egeria, the secret inspirer of all this country's disasters.

THE PORTER [*suddenly, in an unjustifiably sharp voice, to two more of the travellers*]: The next two, please, go along, in there. What are you waiting for?

[*The two travellers go out. Only the* PORTER, *the* ENGINEER, *the* TRAVELLER, ARGIA, *and the* PEASANT-WOMAN *are left.*]

THE PORTER [*to the* ENGINEER]: I . . . I hate that woman, too, of course. I hate her more than you do.

THE TRAVELLER [*as though to himself*]: All the same, she must have had *some* sort of sway over people.

THE PORTER: People who talk about her say she . . . did seem very proud and haughty, but at the same time . . . sincere. They say people could never bring themselves to tell lies to her.

THE TRAVELLER [*with detachment*]: The only human needs she ever seems to have acknowledged were the ones that can be reconciled with a dignified and honourable idea of the world. Everything she did and said was, as it were, essential and refined. It must be costing her a great deal to stay in hiding.

THE ENGINEER: Forgive my asking: but did any of you ever see her in those days? [*To* ORAZIO.] Did you?

THE PORTER: No.

THE ENGINEER: Have you ever spoken to anybody who'd ever seen her?

THE PORTER: No.

THE ENGINEER: You see, then? It's all popular ignorance: a spirit of opposition prepared to raise even a ghost against the idea of progress, if it can.

THE TRAVELLER: It's a very remarkable ghost, then. [*A pause.*] I'd like to meet it.

[RAIM *bursts into the room.*]

RAIM: I'd like to know what you all think you're doing? You take all this very calmly, don't you? The general has been sighted.

THE TRAVELLER [*calmly*]: Indeed?

RAIM [*to the* PORTER]: You, quick, take all these people in there; try and fix them up in there somehow . . . [*To* ARGIA.] No, not you. You wait in here. There are some things I have to ask you.

[*The* ENGINEER, *the* TRAVELLER, *and the* PEASANT-WOMAN *go out into the next room, at a sign from the* PORTER. *The* PORTER *picks up their documents, which have been left on a table.*]

RAIM [*severely, to* ARGIA]: And in particular I should like to know what are the exact and precise reasons . . . the, ah, the reasons why you have undertaken this journey up here.

ARGIA [*adopting the same official tone*]: Personal reasons.

[*The* PORTER *is on his way out of the room.*]

RAIM: What were they? I may as well say that it will be as well for you if you explain them in detail.

[*The door closes behind the* PORTER.]

ARGIA [*slowly dropping the official tone*]: The reasons in detail were as follows: I was getting horribly miserable down in Rosad, my darling, and I didn't know what to do.

RAIM: I suppose you think it's very clever, coming up here?

ARGIA: They told me you were up in the mountains.

RAIM: What do you want with me?

ARGIA: So now you've joined up with the Unitary Party, Raim? Clever boy. Are you fighting? Shooting people?

RAIM: I asked you what you'd come for.

ARGIA: Nothing. You should have seen your face when you saw me. I could have died laughing. Have I upset you?

RAIM [*harshly*]: Not at all, I was very glad to see you.

ARGIA: I wonder what your present bosses would say if anyone told them who the ones before were.

RAIM: That's not the sort of thing *you* can feel particularly easy about. When did you leave?

ARGIA: Yesterday.

RAIM: Have you any money?

ARGIA: . . . A certain amount.

RAIM [*sarcastically*]: Yes, I dare say.

ARGIA: I sold everything I had. Not that it fetched much.

RAIM: My dear girl, this is the very last place you should have come to. I only managed to get fixed up here by a miracle. I've had to tell them the most incredible tales. You needn't think I'm going to start running any risks, now.

ARGIA: I will make you run risks, Raim.

RAIM: No, my dear, we're a bit too near Rosad for that. I've enough risks of my own to run; too many. You're a woman, you always get along somehow. But those bloody fools up here, they suspect everybody. The slightest thing, and they're foaming at the mouth. I want to come through all this mess alive. And rich. Yes. What you want up here is a good memory: for afterwards. That's all you want: it'll be a good investment. One side's going to come out on top after all this; and if you've been robbing and betraying and murdering on that side you'll be a hero; if you've done the same for the other you'll be ruined. And there are so many people living in fear and trembling, I've decided to be one of the landed gentry in my old age. If it's anyhow possible you and I can meet up again in the spring. May I ask why you came up here to find me? [*Sarcastically.*] Do you love me? Did you miss me down there?

ARGIA: Raim: I really didn't know what to do. The other day, the police arrested me.

RAIM: Why?

ARGIA: They were just rounding people up. I hadn't done anything. I was in a café on one of the avenues. It's difficult now, being a woman on your own.

RAIM: So what?

ARGIA: Oh, nothing. I was actually rather a success at the police-station. I had to stay the night there to start with; but the superintendent was quite kind to me in the morning. He told me to ring up someone who'd vouch for me. Raim: it was then I realized something for the first time: I don't really know anybody. I know people: but they're only Christian names or nicknames, as a rule. I hardly know anybody by their surname. And now, with all this confusion, so-and-so run away, so-and-so dead . . . There I was, with the telephone-book, turning over the pages . . . and I could think of no one.

RAIM: So what?

ARGIA: They questioned me about my means of subsistence. The result was I was given repatriation notice. The superintendent told me I had to be decentralized, whatever that is. He said they'd send me away the next day with a military escort. 'All right,' I said: 'but I'll have to pack my bags.' They sent me home with a guard. I gave the guard my watch, and he pretended to lose me in the crowd. There were no trams, of course; the streets were all blocked; soldiers everywhere; 'no stopping here'. And so on. Finally, I managed to get a seat on a lorry; the price was sheer robbery. It was raining, my feet were hurting, my clothes were soaking wet; do you know what I felt like, Raim? A rat, a drowned rat. Then at Bled they made us détour, then again at Nova. Inspections. And then more inspections; hold-ups; bayonets. At Sestan they stole my coat. It hasn't been easy getting up here. I'm lucky I've found you so soon. [She has seated herself on his knee.]

RAIM [getting up]: I'm sorry, my dear, but the people here mustn't know I know you. I'm speaking for your own good as well as mine.

ARGIA: Raim, I couldn't stay down there. I was frightened; can't you understand? Not that they can really charge me with anything. But everywhere you go . . . [with a sudden cry, which she quickly suppresses] you see the gallows, Raim. Just because of stray accusations . . . or vague resemblances, rows of people have been hanged . . .

RAIM: And you think that's going to encourage me to keep you here? I've as much cause to be worried as you have. It would be madness just to slap our worries together. No, Argia, no: everyone has to look after himself; I want to finish this war above ground, not underneath.

ARGIA [after a pause, with an effort to make it seem unimportant]: Raim: what if I told you . . . that I'd really . . . missed you?

RAIM: That's what I said. You love me. I've bewitched you.

ARGIA: Oh, I know you're quite right to laugh at me. [Lightly imploring him.] But . . . when we're both together I feel . . . a bit safer . . . I was happy, when I saw you; don't you understand?

RAIM: Well, I wasn't, see? I wasn't.

ARGIA: Raim . . .

RAIM: My dear . . . I've no intention of burdening myself with you. Besides, you'll be sure to find a way out, I know you. [*Shrugging his shoulders.*] There aren't many women round here. They're in great demand.

ARGIA [*lowers her eyes for a moment; then looks at him and says, in low quiet tones*]: What a disgusting creature you are, aren't you, Raim? I sometimes think you must be the nastiest person in the world.

RAIM: Ah, now you're talking sense. You go away and leave me, my dear; I'm not worthy of you. I'd feel guilty at keeping you here.

ARGIA: And to think that *I* am running after somebody like *you*, begging . . . from *you*. It's enough to make one weep; or laugh.

RAIM: Well, you laugh, then, my dear. Let's both have a good laugh, and say good-bye. You'd be wasted on me. You know, Argia, one of the reasons you don't attract me is your silly games of make-believe the whole time. You've always tried to act so very grand. With me! The superior lady, always disgusted, so easily offended. You of all people! Always behaving as though dirt was something that only belonged to other people.

ARGIA [*her eyes lowered*]: No, Raim, that's not true.

RAIM: While the truth is that if ever there was a filthy creature in the world, you're it.

ARGIA: I'm sorry, Raim, if I spoke like that . . . It's only because deep down I love you, and want to . . .

RAIM: You let me finish. I'm not angry; not at all. But you may as well get this straight. You see, Argia: you're not only a dead weight on me . . . It's not only that. You've begun to get rather too many wrinkles for my liking . . .

ARGIA [*trying to turn the whole thing into a jest*]: Really, Raim? A few minutes ago, when they were all talking about the Queen, did you know they all looked at me? They half thought I was the Queen.

RAIM: You! The Queen? They've only got to look at you to see what *you* are. The Queen. There isn't a square inch about you that's decent.

ARGIA [*with another hoarse effort at playfulness*]: Be quiet, Raim, if you don't, I'll bite you! [*She takes his hand.*]

RAIM [*freeing himself with a brutal jerk which makes her stagger backwards*]: You leave me alone. Don't try and pretend I'm joking. What you ought to do, my dear, is to go and stand in front of your looking-glass and say to yourself as often as you can: 'I'm a cheap, low, dirty slut.' You've never done a decent thing in your whole life. [*Deliberately.*] Smell of the bed. Cigarette-smoke. Wandering about the room with nothing on, whistling. That's you. And there have been one or two unsavoury episodes which even suggest that the secret police made use of you. Oh, make no mistake, I'm not the kind of man who's easily prejudiced. But you, Argia, quite apart from everything else, you're cheap. The little bogus middle-class girlie, who's read a few books. Even in your intrigues you're small and petty: the little tart with the furnished rooms and the pawnshop tickets: I've been getting fed up with you now for quite a long time, see? Well: it's over. I'm not going through all that again.

ARGIA [*her eyes lowered; and with a faint wail*]: Raim, I've nowhere to go.

RAIM: Then go to hell. It's the one place . . . [*His voice suddenly reassumes its official tone. He has heard footsteps coming.*] It's absolutely necessary for . . . for political reasons. And even if you have to stay here tonight, it's no great disaster. You and the other woman, that peasant-woman, can stay in here. The other passengers in the other rooms. It'll be all right. I'll see about finding some blankets for you. Political and military necessities, unfortunately. It isn't my fault.

[*It is the* TRAVELLER *who has come in.* RAIM *has turned to him on his last words. The* TRAVELLER *approaches amiably.*]

THE TRAVELLER: Nor ours either. I seem to get the impression that you, too, regard these . . . these military and political necessities, with a certain amount of scepticism.

RAIM [*looks at him for a moment: and then says, also amiably*]: Bless my soul, that's exactly what I was saying to . . . [*To* ARGIA, *sharply.*] You may withdraw, madam. Go in there with the others.

[ARGIA *goes out.*]

RAIM [*amiably but cautiously*]: Yes, I was just saying that . . . well, of course, I'm a good revolutionary and all that (we all are, of course), but I . . . understand things. I know how to put myself in another man's place. Unfortunate travellers . . . perhaps even important men, well-to-do, plenty of money and so on, suddenly finding themselves . . .

THE TRAVELLER: Reduced to hoping for a blanket!

RAIM [*carefully feeling his way*]: I'm afraid I may have seemed a little bit ... official with you just now. I had to be, of course. You understand.

THE TRAVELLER: I have the feeling that you too understand ...

RAIM: Oh, at once, my dear friend, straight away. I'll be happy to be of any help, if it's at all possible ...

THE TRAVELLER: The secret is to regard these things with a certain amount of detachment; don't you agree?

RAIM: Definitely. You know, I got the impression, when we were talking here a few minutes ago, that you too ... feel a certain distaste for some of the excesses that ...

THE TRAVELLER: Ah, you noticed that, did you?

RAIM: Oh, but of course! I'm a man ... who doesn't feel so very bitter as all that towards your *own* ideals, you know, sir.

THE TRAVELLER: Is that so? I'm delighted to hear it.

RAIM [*mysteriously*]: I'm too much in contact with the new chiefs the whole time, of course.

THE TRAVELLER [*shaking his head*]: And they ...

RAIM [*laughing*]: ... aren't so terribly different from the old ones.

THE TRAVELLER: That was to be expected.

RAIM: Once you ignore the individual differences of character, you find they raise their voices, ring the bell, upset people and shoot 'em ...

THE TRAVELLER: ... in exactly the same way as the others. Yes. I assume you were also in the habit of hobnobbing with the former high-ups?

RAIM: Oh, no, God forbid. I had to put up with them. And now I have to put up with these. 'Put up!' It's all very sad.

THE TRAVELLER: Especially for men of intelligence. [*As though speaking to himself.*] Who really ought to be looking after themselves.

RAIM [*warmly*]: Exactly! That's just what I say. These disturbances ought to be a godsend for people with any imagination ...! [*He has taken a bottle out of its hiding-place, and is pouring out a drink for himself and the* TRAVELLER.] 'Ought to be looking after themselves.' Yes. As you say. Look after yourself, what? You know, I have a theory about all these things.

THE TRAVELLER: I'd like to hear it.

RAIM: There are two kinds of people in this world: the people who eat beef-steaks and the people who eat potatoes. Whose fault is it? Because it's certainly not true that the millionaire eats a hundred thousand beef-steaks.

THE TRAVELLER [*drinking*]: He'd soon have indigestion if he did.

RAIM [*also drinking*]: He eats half a beef-steak and helps it down with a dose of bicarbonate. Yes. Then why do all these other poor devils have to make do with potatoes? It's simple. There aren't enough beef-steaks to go round. The limitation on the number of beef-steaks in the world is a profound inconvenience on which social reforms have not the slightest influence. Not the slightest. Now, it follows from this that whatever régime you're under, the number of eaters of beef-steak . . .

THE TRAVELLER: Remains constant.

RAIM: Exactly. And the wonderful thing is that the beef-steak eaters are always the same people. They may *look* different, of course. But who are they?

THE TRAVELLER: The bosses . . .

RAIM: . . . and the wide-boys. It's always the same act; the palaces and the armchairs are always there, and it's always by virtue of the people and the potatoes that the high-ups can sit in the palaces eating their beef-steaks. That being agreed, what's the logical thing to do? It's to belong, whatever happens, to . . .

THE TRAVELLER: The beef-steak party.

RAIM: It's not for everybody, of course. It requires intelligence . . . intuition. [*With sudden firmness.*] You'll forgive me, sir, but I don't believe in equality; except over toothpicks. It's only by climbing up and down that we keep fit. [*Gently.*] I believe in money.

THE TRAVELLER: You're not the only one.

RAIM: If man had never developed that great vision of having a bank account, he'd never have emerged from cave-life.

THE TRAVELLER [*solemnly*]: Progress. Progress.

RAIM: A little bit of salt on the tail. Just think what a colossal bore it'd all be otherwise. Everybody stuck there as though in a morgue. A row of coffins. If a man's a hunchback, he's always a hunchback. We all know that. If a man's ugly, he's ugly. If he's a fool, he's a fool. But at any rate, however common and unfortunate a man may be, he can always hope to get rich, little by little. Rich. Which means he won't be ugly any more, nor a fool . . .

THE TRAVELLER: Nor even a hunchback.

RAIM: That's your *real* democracy; your real progress. Yes, that's why it's the duty, the absolute duty of every intelligent man ... [*his voice changes once more and becomes peremptory and severe; footsteps are approaching*] to fight and to strive! To fight and strive in the service of our flag and our republic! [*He turns to see who is coming in: and is at once thrown into great agitation.*] Good God, it's you, General Biante, forgive me, I never saw you come in! [*He runs to the door.*] How are you? Are you feeling a little better?

> [*BIANTE has entered, supported by an armed guard, MAUPA, who at once helps him to sit down. BIANTE is a hirsute man in civilian clothes. His shoulders, neck, and one arm are voluminously bandaged, and compel him to move stiffly. He looks first at RAIM, then at the TRAVELLER, and then turns back to RAIM.*

BIANTE [*his voice is low and hoarse*]: What are you doing?

RAIM [*eagerly*]: Nothing, general, I was just interrogating a traveller.

BIANTE: Oh. Good. And what did the traveller have to say to you?

THE TRAVELLER [*sweetly*]: We were discussing some rather curious offers of help he'd just been making to me.

RAIM: I? General Biante! [*He sniggers.*] I was just holding out a little bait, just wriggling a little hook about. I ought to say that this gentleman seems to me a very suspicious character. I think we should do well to point out to Commissar Amos ...

BIANTE [*between his teeth, not amused*]: Don't be a bloody fool.

RAIM: ... the minute the commissar arrives.

THE TRAVELLER [*calmly, to RAIM*]: I arrived an hour ago. I am Commissar Amos. How are you, Biante?

BIANTE: Haven't you managed to get me a doctor?

AMOS: Not yet.

BIANTE: I'd be damned glad of one. I come through the whole war safely: and what do I have to be wiped out by? A stray bullet. Amos, I'm swollen right up to the neck; my fingers feel like sausages. I wouldn't like to die, Amos. I'd like to live and see the new age in. Do you think I'm getting gangrene?

AMOS [*calmly*]: Let's hope not.

BIANTE [*suddenly to RAIM, hysterically*]: Go and find a doctor, for Christ's sake! You filthy bastard, go and find a doctor! And send all those people in here!

[RAIM *rushes out.*]

BIANTE [*breathing laboriously*]: The Queen's here! Somewhere: in our midst. Nobody's doing anything. Nobody knows anything. And yet they're all saying it! The Queen's here!

AMOS [*calmly*]: Yes, I'd heard for certain she was.

BIANTE: Good God. Who from?

AMOS: They stopped a man on the road from Bled. He was coming up here to meet her.

BIANTE: Where is he?

AMOS: He was too quick for us. While they were bringing him here he poisoned himself. So as not to have to acknowledge his accomplice.

BIANTE [*almost a whisper*]: The Queen's here! Alive!

MAUPA [*suddenly, from the background, without moving, in a kind of ecstasy*]: We want to see the colour of the Queen's entrails.

[RAIM *is escorting the travellers into the room.*]

MAUPA [*continuing without pause*]: All our troubles come from the Queen. If our sick are covered with wounds, if our children grow up crippled and our daughters shameless, the Queen's to blame, no one else. [*His voice gets gradually louder.*] If she falls into my hands, I'll keep her dying slowly for three whole days. I'll make them hear her screams from the mountain-tops. I'll slit her up bit by bit till she lies there wide open like a peach. The thought that the Queen is near makes my hair stand on end like a wild boar's. We must find her.

AMOS [*calmly*]: She will be found soon enough. The road up here has been blocked since this morning, but the number of road passengers they've stopped hasn't been very large. This very night we shall begin to go over them methodically.

BIANTE [*turning to the others, who are standing huddled together in the background*]: Yes, you there! It's you we're talking about! [*Shouting and getting up from his chair.*] I'm here: General Biante. I assume full powers ... together with Commissar Amos here ... Is there anybody here who's a doctor? No? Blast you. [*Brief pause.*] You're all under arrest! No one's to move an inch from where you are now.

AMOS: The exits are all guarded; the guards have orders to shoot.

BIANTE: You'll all be questioned. So look out! You'll be detained here till further orders! [*Pointing.*] The women in there; the men in here. Get on with it, everyone to his proper place. [*He moves towards the door.*]

AMOS [*calmly, for the pleasure of contradicting him*]: The men will go in there; the women will stay in here.

[BIANTE *casts a sharp glance at* AMOS, *and goes out, supported by* MAUPA.

The travellers have all gone out again except ARGIA *and the* PEASANT-WOMAN.]

AMOS [*also on his way out, turns in the doorway*]: Good night for the present. [*He goes out.*]

[ARGIA *stands for a moment looking at the door, and then shrugs her shoulders.*]

ARGIA: What a lot of stupid nonsense! The result is that we sleep in here. Let's hope the interpreter remembers to bring us some blankets. There was a sofa in that other room too. [*She points to the next room.*] I'm very tired, aren't you? [*She sits.*] What a lot of clowns they all are. Let's hope they let us sleep till tomorrow morning. [*She begins to fumble in her hand-bag, and brings out a small pot; she takes some cold cream on one finger and dabs it on her face. To the* PEASANT-WOMAN, *who is still seated in the background.*] I suppose in the country you don't go in for this sort of thing? I have to, every night: I'm not so young as I was, I've just been told; it would be asking for trouble if I didn't look after myself. [*She massages her face.*] I suppose I must look a sight with this grease all over my face? Sorry. [*She thinks for a moment.*] I find it rather humiliating being a woman. Even rather humiliating being alive. [*She massages her face.*] You spit in a blackguard's face, and even as you do it, you know perfectly well the only thing to do is to make him go to bed with you ... I'm sorry: but we're both women, after all. I don't mean one really wants to, even. It's all so squalid and humiliating. [*She breaks off.*]

[RAIM *crosses the stage and goes out.*]

ARGIA: I've come a long, long way just to go to bed with a man. [*Pause.*] Making a fuss of a man to try and find out if he's in a good mood or not. Very amusing. [*Pause.*] The trouble is having no money either. Let's hope after we're dead there'll be nothing of that to worry about. [*Turning to the* PEASANT-WOMAN.] Do you mind my asking dear: I suppose you haven't a bit bigger mirror than this? What ... what's the matter? Aren't you feeling all right?

THE PEASANT-WOMAN [*almost inaudibly*]: Yes ...

ARGIA [*going over to her*]: Why, you're covered with sweat. Do you feel ill? You look as if you're going to faint.

THE PEASANT-WOMAN: No ... no. ... [*She sways.*]

ARGIA [*supporting her*]: Did what the brute in here said about the Queen frighten you? You mustn't take any notice of that, it's nothing to do with us ...

[*She breaks off; lets the woman go; and stares at her. The woman stares back at her with wide-open eyes; then she rises, slowly.*]

ARGIA [*after a long pause, in a different voice*]: Is there anything you want?

THE PEASANT-WOMAN: No ... no ...

ARGIA: You could go and lie down in there, on the sofa. Where is your bag?

[*The* PEASANT-WOMAN *grips her bag, as though frightened by* ARGIA's *words.*]

ARGIA: What have you got in there?

THE PEASANT-WOMAN: Some bread ...

ARGIA: Well, my dear, you go in there. Lie down. You'll soon feel better.

[ARGIA *helps the woman into the next room. After a moment she returns, and walks about for a moment or two, perplexed and thoughtful. Suddenly she runs to the other door, opens it and calls in a stifled whisper.*]

ARGIA: Raim! Raim! [*She comes back, and waits.*]

RAIM [*enters: in a whisper*]: What d'you want? Are you mad?

ARGIA [*whispers*]: I'm rich, Raim. I'm worth marrying now. Look at me: I'm a splendid match.

RAIM: What's the matter?

ARGIA: Rich, Raim. Rich. We'll be able to stay in the grandest hotels.

RAIM: What do you mean?

ARGIA: I've discovered the Queen. [*She points towards the next room.*]

RAIM: But there's only that peasant-woman in there.

[ARGIA *nods.*]

CURTAIN

ACT TWO

Only a few moments have passed since the end of the preceding scene. ARGIA *and* RAIM *are speaking rapidly, in low voices.*

RAIM [*sweating and agitated*]: God damn the day I ever met you! You're the cause of all my troubles. This is a frightful thing . . . it's terribly dangerous.

ARGIA [*mockingly*]: Well, why not go to Amos and Biante, then, and tell *them* about it? Tell them the Queen's here; with a heavy bag.

RAIM: Yes, and you know what they'll do? Kill me; and you too. So that they can have the credit . . . and the bag as well. It's a murder-factory up here. Their only aim here is to kill people. Yes: accidentally; for amusement.

ARGIA: Then we'd better forget about it, that's all.

RAIM: I could box your ears! This is the first piece of luck I've ever had in the whole of my life. It's my big chance. I shall go mad if I have to let this slip through my fingers.

ARGIA: Well, don't let it, then.

RAIM: God, I'm frightened of this. A rifle can go off all by itself up here. Damn the whole bloody world! But are you sure about this, Argia? You've always been half-crazy; you imagine things the whole time.

ARGIA: I'm quite certain. We looked at one another. It was just a flicker. And then I saw. And she saw that I saw. She was almost fainting.

RAIM: The devil is there's not a minute to lose. What was this bag like?

ARGIA: Small, but quite heavy.

RAIM: Gold; diamonds. It'll kill me. You couldn't get a needle out of this place. Bury it; come back later: some hopes! They're more likely to bury me. [*In a burst of anger.*] I'm the one who's in danger, can't you see?

ARGIA: But I can help you. I can do it for you.

RAIM: Yes. You're a woman, of course. You know her . . . You've already been talking to her . . . But, mind, it would have to look as if it were your own idea. Something you'd thought of yourself. How did she seem?

ARGIA: Terrified.

RAIM: Yes, that's the way to go about it, obviously. Try and frighten her. She'll give you the bag herself, without even being asked.

ARGIA: We mustn't bother too much about the bag, Raim.

RAIM: Why not?

ARGIA: We couldn't be seen with it; and it would be difficult to take it away, or bury it.

RAIM: Well, what, then?

ARGIA: The names.

RAIM: What do you mean, for God's sake, what names?

ARGIA: Thé names: of her friends. There's sure to be a whole gang round her. Big, important people.

RAIM: By God! You clever piece! [*He kisses her.*] Do you think she'd talk?

ARGIA: We can try and persuade her to. Her life's in our hands.

RAIM: You could manage that all right, if you frightened her. But what then?

ARGIA: We won't take the bag away with us. We'll take the names. In our heads.

RAIM: Yes, but surely we could try and get the bag as well? And what if we got the names?

ARGIA: Well, from then on there'd be quite a number of people who might be feeling extremely uneasy . . .

RAIM [*completing the sentence*]: . . . and every so often the tax-collector would drop in and see them. Yes. Me. 'Excuse me, Your Excellency, you won't forget the usual donation, will you? Though only, of course, if you're interested in surviving a little longer . . . Yes?' My God, what a game! No. No. No! It's too dangerous. It's a good idea, but sooner or later, they'd have me done in. Don't you see? [*With bitter nastiness.*] The bastards would soon be sparing *me* the afflictions of old age, don't worry! No, no, Argia, we must try and grab what we can out of it, quickly. Jewels, rubies, and so on . . . [*He suddenly lowers his voice.*] God, here she is. Go on: see what you can do.

[*The* QUEEN *has opened the door, and stands looking, as though hypnotized, at* ARGIA; RAIM *casts a glance at her and goes out in silence.*]

ARGIA: Did you want something?

THE QUEEN [*breathing painfully*]: No ... no ... I only wanted ...

ARGIA: To come and talk to me for a bit? Is that it?

THE QUEEN: I ... saw that perhaps ... you have a kind heart ...

ARGIA: Well ... that always depends how God made us, doesn't it? Come over here, my dear. Come on. I wanted to talk to you as well. You're a country-woman, aren't you?

THE QUEEN [*almost inaudibly*]: Yes ...

ARGIA: I'm fond of country-people. Do you actually go out in the fields?

THE QUEEN: Yes ...

ARGIA: What do you do there?

THE QUEEN: I work ...

ARGIA: Digging? Hoeing?

[*The* QUEEN *holds out her hands appealingly.*]

ARGIA: Yes, they're real peasant's hands, aren't they? Good girl. It can't be easy to get your hands like that. It must take a long time. And a good deal of hard work. A good deal of digging and hoeing.

THE QUEEN: Yes ...

ARGIA: Are you all by yourself?

THE QUEEN: Yes ...

ARGIA: I can see you're very frightened; I think you've every reason to be. It was sensible of you to come to me. As a matter of fact, I could probably help you. And in return you could perhaps be kind enough to do something for me.

THE QUEEN: I ... don't know what sort of thing ... you mean.

ARGIA [*almost a whisper*]: My dear friend, your name isn't Elisabetta by any chance, I suppose?

[*There is a long silence.*]

THE QUEEN [*she can scarcely speak*]: No.

ARGIA: Odd. I thought it was, somehow ... However. [*She raises her voice slightly.*] You're quite sure your name is not Elisabetta?

THE QUEEN: No ... no ... no ... [*She again holds out her hands.*]

ARGIA [*a little louder still*]: You insist on denying that your name is ...

THE QUEEN [*interrupting her with a gesture*]: My bag is there. You can have it. I thought you'd want it. [*She points.*] I've hidden it. You can take it whenever you want to.

ARGIA: Hidden it where?

THE QUEEN: In there. Up above the rafters, in the corner.

ARGIA: Is there much in it?

THE QUEEN: Only what I have left. It's hidden in the bread. There are three little loaves.

ARGIA: It's not really much of a sacrifice for you, is it? If you ever come to the top again, it'll be a mere trifle to you. And if you don't, it's all up with you anyway. But it would be a godsend to me. You see, I'm poor; I'm hag-ridden with debts . . . [*She breaks off.*]

RAIM [*coming in quickly*]: Excuse me, ladies! I've just remembered about the blankets . . . I came to see if . . . [*He goes up to* ARGIA, *and speaks to her under his breath, almost with fury.*] I've been thinking. I want the names as well. I want everything. [*Retreating.*] I'll bring you the blankets, in half a minute. [*He goes out.*]

ARGIA: Yes, you've shown a good deal of common sense. Well, you'll have to show a little more now. The situation is very simple. I can either go out of that door and call a soldier. Or I can keep my mouth shut, and help you. I've a friend here; you just saw him. But I'm afraid it means sharing things out, your majesty. We're sisters now. Everything in common. I'd be a fool to be satisfied with the leavings in the middle of three small loaves, wouldn't I?

THE QUEEN [*almost inaudibly*]: I've nothing else.

ARGIA: For year after year you used to walk on marble and sleep in silk. I've not had quite such a good time. The moment's come to level things up.

THE QUEEN: I swear to you I've nothing else.

ARGIA: That's not true. You still have friends. People working for you. I want them to be my friends as well. I want them to help me. *I* want people I can rely on, too. Do you see what I mean?

THE QUEEN: Yes . . .

ARGIA: In any case, the people I mean are hard-boiled enough. They're the people who've shoved you into all this mess. It was they who drove you out of your hiding-place.

THE QUEEN: No, no, there wasn't anybody.

ARGIA: Your friends.

THE QUEEN: I haven't any.

ARGIA: Come, come, you won't be doing *them* any harm. The only trouble they'll have is helping me a little in these hard times. Your friends.

THE QUEEN [*imploring*]: They're all dead, they've all been killed. I'm alone now.

ARGIA: Your majesty, you used to sweep down red-carpeted stair-cases; the ones I had to climb weren't half so pretty. But even they taught me things. I learned . . . a good deal. You'll be very silly if you try to fool *me*.

THE QUEEN: Oh, please have pity . . .

ARGIA: I'm hardened, your majesty. I'm indifferent even to my own misfortunes by now; you can imagine how I feel about yours. [*Almost shouting.*] Come on, tell me who they are: who are your friends? Who are they? [*She breaks off.*]

[*The* QUEEN *has taken from her bosom a piece of paper; she offers it to* ARGIA.]

ARGIA [*before taking it*]: They're there?

THE QUEEN: Yes.

ARGIA [*taking the paper*]: A good many stories about you are going the rounds. I thought I should have to insist much harder. You're rather meek and mild, for a Queen, aren't you? [*She looks at the paper.*] Darling, you must take me for an idiot. A list of them, all ready? Just like that?

THE QUEEN: Yes.

ARGIA: You've been carrying it about on you?

THE QUEEN: Yes.

ARGIA [*sarcastically condescending*]: Why, my dear, why?

THE QUEEN: Because I'm frightened.

ARGIA: Of what?

THE QUEEN [*desperately*]: Of being tortured. I've heard of them doing . . . terrible . . . dreadful things . . . And I'm frightened; don't you understand? [*Overcome for a moment.*] The thought of it is driving me insane! [*Controlling herself.*] I'd have been bound to tell them in the end just the same . . . And if there was this paper . . . They'd have found it on me; it would all have been simple. Oh, please believe me, I beg of you, please. It's the truth.

ARGIA [*looks at the paper*]: So these are the ones? Your faithful friends. The people who are risking their lives for you.

THE QUEEN: Yes.

ARGIA [*dropping her voice*]: But are you really the 'Queen'?

THE QUEEN: Yes . . . Except that I . . . lost whatever courage I had, in that cellar, at Bielovice. Please: I've nothing else to give you now. I hope you'll save me . . . I hope you and your friend will help me to escape . . .

    [RAIM *enters quickly with a couple of blankets.*]

RAIM: Here you are, ladies, the blankets! [*He throws them on a chair; to the* QUEEN.] Do you mind? [*He takes the paper from* ARGIA'S *hand, and draws her aside. He looks at the card, and says quietly.*] It's so stupid and childish it's bound to be true. [*He stares at the paper hard: then puts it under* ARGIA'S *eyes.*] You fix these four names in your head as well.

ARGIA: Yes.

RAIM: Good. Have you got them? You're sure?

ARGIA: Yes.

RAIM: So have I. [*He lights a match and sets the paper alight; to the* QUEEN.] Madam, we have to think of our safety as well, though our methods may be a bit different. [*He stamps on the ashes hysterically.*]

ARGIA [*a whisper*]: Do you think it's possible to get her away?

RAIM [*a whisper*]: It's not only possible, it's indispensable. And it's not only indispensable, it's not enough. Escape isn't enough. There's something else as well.

ARGIA: What?

RAIM [*rapidly*]: If she gets across the mountains and gets in touch with those people [*he points to the ashes*] it'll go very hard with us. And if she doesn't, it'll be even worse: they'll catch her; and she'll tell everything. And if we leave her here, when they question her tomorrow, she'll talk just the same. She'll give us away. I'd be a madman to risk my life – and yours – on a damn silly thing like that.

ARGIA: What then?

RAIM: We've got to make *sure* she keeps her mouth shut.

ARGIA [*has understood*]: No!

RAIM: It's the best thing for her too, in a way. If those two in there find her, her last minutes aren't going to be very enviable. She's finished now, either way. Better for her it should all be over quickly without frightening her.

ARGIA: No, no.

RAIM [*in an excited whisper*]: Do you think I like it? Our lives depend on this. We can't back out now, it's too late. We oughtn't to have started it. Darling, it's got to be done.

ARGIA [*horrified*]: Got to? And do you think *I* . . .

RAIM: It's always you, isn't it? Whose idea was it? Yours. You got me into this danger. You arranged it all. And now it's not nice enough for you. You're worse than anybody. No, my dear. It's got to be done. And we're in it together.

ARGIA [*with horrified resignation*]: Have you thought . . . how?

RAIM: I'm thinking now. [*Moving away and speaking louder.*] I'll be back in a few minutes, madam. We're looking after you. [*He goes out.*]

THE QUEEN: Does he intend to help me?

ARGIA [*without looking at her*]: Yes.

THE QUEEN: Your friend will get me away?

ARGIA: Yes.

THE QUEEN [*suddenly, torn with anguish*]: For pity's sake, don't let them hurt me, don't betray me, for pity's sake . . . [*She darts forward and takes* ARGIA'S *hand as though to kiss it.*]

ARGIA [*almost angrily, tearing her hand away*]: What are you doing? What's the matter with you?

THE QUEEN [*desperately*]: Oh, my God, you're deceiving me, everybody deceives me . . . Everybody plays with me like a cat with a mouse . . . I can't go on any longer; oh, God, I'd rather die now . . . I don't want to think any more; call them, call the soldiers, I'll call them myself, kill me, kill me, straight away . . .

ARGIA [*shaking her*]: Stop it, stop it, you silly woman.

[*The* QUEEN *has fallen to her knees and remains there gasping for breath.*]

ARGIA [*exasperated*]: You'll dirty your knees, your majesty. Yes, of course, you'll be saved, you'll be got away. It's important to us as well, isn't it? [*With gloomy hostility.*] In any case, it's dishonourable, it's unfair, to lose your dignity like this. It's against the rules of the game; it embarrasses people. A chambermaid would behave better. I would myself, my dear; I've never squealed like that: like a mouse under a peasant's foot. And I'm not a queen . . . far from it. When you used to give your orders, with the flag flying over the palace, down below, underneath all the people who were obeying you and giving your orders to other people, down below all of them, right down on the pavement, there was I. I didn't drive in a landau; and they'd made a woman of me by the time I was eleven. Your majesty there were some days when I used to feel as if the whole world had wiped their feet on my face. And now you come and slobber all over my hands. No, no, my dear: the silk clothes and the box at the Opera have to be paid for. You heard a few minutes ago, in here, what the people think of you. Your hands have not always been rough. And they've signed a lot of papers in their time.

THE QUEEN: No.

ARGIA: What do you mean: no?

THE QUEEN: I've never done any harm to anyone. It was never left to me to decide anything. Nothing they say of me is true. [*She shudders with horror.*] The only thing that's true is that at Bielovice I was covered with dead bodies and blood. I could feel them dying, on top of me! Since then I've been in perpetual flight. It isn't true that I met the soldiers on the bridge at Nistria. If I had, I should have fainted at their feet. I've not had a single moment free from terror for five years. They've killed almost every one of my friends; but unfortunately not all of them. Every so often one or other of them manages to track me down. I'm running away from my friends even more than from my enemies. What can they want of me any more? I can't do anything, I don't want to do anything, the only thing I know now is fear; I sleep in fear, I dream in fear. I'll never, never do anything again either for anyone or against anyone. I only want to escape, and never see or know anything again. I want to stop being afraid. Nobody can have anything to fear from me. I'll give up everything, rights, titles, I'll forget everything.

ARGIA [*with sombre irony*]: It almost looks as if I'd done you a service in taking your jewels off you. You are abdicating. There are some people who'd be extremely disillusioned if they could hear you.

THE QUEEN: I have nothing and I no longer want anything.

ARGIA: Then why are you making so much fuss? What *do* you want?

THE QUEEN: To be left alive. Nothing else. Unknown; far away. And to sleep, night after night, in peace.

[*The two women turn round.* RAIM *has entered, slowly. He bows slightly to the* QUEEN, *and beckons* ARGIA *aside.*]

RAIM [*whispers*]: The job's going to be taken off our hands. I've found a way out. It's quite respectable, too. This building has two exits: this one, and that one over there. The guard on this one, across the courtyard, will be me. The one on the other, on the wall, is Maupa, that soldier you saw in here. He's a real brute. [*To the* QUEEN.] Yes, this is for you, madam. We are preparing a way out for you. [*To* ARGIA *once more.*] It was easy to persuade that swine that the revolution demanded that he should fire; often; at sight; the first squeak of a door or movement in the shadows. Even me, if I tried to: if I opened that door, I'd be opening my own way to hell. But that I shan't do. In a few minutes' time you'll hear a signal: the hoot of an owl. The Queen will say good-bye to you, and come out through this door. Our hands will be as white as snow.

ARGIA [*horrified*]: And if the shot doesn't kill her?

RAIM [*gloomy, subdued*]: In that case, I . . . [*He breaks off.*] It would be just reckless cowardice to leave the thing half-done. What should I get out of that? The only profit there, would be for my dead bones, because it's obvious the Queen would talk and I'd lose my life. But if a dead man's bones know nothing about profit and loss, do you think stupidity and superstition are going to hold my hand back? Why light candles if your prayers mean nothing? [*He blows to left and right as though to put out two imaginary candles burning before a non-existent shrine.*] They're all wolves: why should I be a lamb? Plenty of good people are dying in these hard times, one more or less makes no odds. They say the Bible stories prophesy a bath of blood for the earth. But in practice it needs gallons, especially when you see how much the earth soaks up. Besides, I suffer from poor health; I've got to make sure of some sort of a future. [*He returns to the subject.*] So if anything goes wrong . . . Oh, why does this woman get people into such a mess instead of doing away with herself? Her life's useless and wretched and short, anyway. Better for her to finish here than run about, being smelt out like a hare the whole time, always in fear and trembling. [*To* ARGIA.] If anything does go wrong, as soon as I hear the shots, I shall run round through the courtyard . . . and if the soldier's shots haven't been enough . . . I'll finish it off myself . . . Let's hope it won't be necessary. Quickly, now. I shall be glad when it's all over. [*He makes a slight bow to the* QUEEN *and goes out.*]

ARGIA [*avoids looking at the* QUEEN]: Madam, you must be very brave now, this is going to be very dangerous for all of us. But I think you'll be all right.

THE QUEEN: I am ready.

ARGIA [*breathing heavily*]: What has to be done, has to. That's true, isn't it? If you want to escape . . .

THE QUEEN: Go on.

ARGIA: They've found a man who's willing to accompany you up the hidden paths as far as the frontier. In a few minutes we shall hear a signal. Then you'll go out, through that door over there. Outside, you'll find the man who's willing to take you on your way. You'll have nothing more to worry about.

THE QUEEN [*her hands clasped*]: Oh, my dear. Your sweet face and your gentle voice will stay in my heart till the last day of my life, and beyond. Yes, surely beyond; so that when I meet you again in heaven, I can run to you, crying . . . [*She takes* ARGIA'S *hands.*] 'Bright soul! My dear, dear sister! Do you remember me? It is I. And now we are together because on that day we had to part so soon.'

[ARGIA *tries to push her away.*]

THE QUEEN: Don't push me away from you; oh, please let me stay like this for a moment. [*She laughs.*] Treat me like a frightened animal who has sought refuge in your lap. That does happen sometimes. Hold me and stroke me. [*She clasps* ARGIA *tightly.*] What is your name?

ARGIA: Argia.

THE QUEEN: I feel as if I were being re-born, here, in your arms. [*She starts.*] What's that? Was it the signal?

ARGIA: No, not yet.

THE QUEEN: But please tell me: are you sure the man who is going to come with me up the mountain is really to be trusted? Can I really be sure of him? When we get to one of those dark gullies in the hills, he won't leap at me and cut my throat, will he?

ARGIA: No. No.

THE QUEEN: Don't, don't think I don't trust you. It's only that it is so difficult to shake off the terror. Through the whole of these years I've been haunted by only one single thought: the horrible tortures they do . . . My God, they put people to inhuman horrors: did you know that? I have a poison with me . . . but I can never be sure if I shall be able to swallow it in time. I always used to imagine that dreadful moment: a man looking at me . . . turning round to look at me . . . then a glint in his eye . . . and I was recognized . . . lost. That's why I've . . . oh, dearest Argia, please forgive me! But you said yourself we were women together . . . [*Whispers.*] Sometimes a man has stared hard at me . . . a peasant, or a herdsman, or a woodman . . . I've given myself to him! Given myself! I'm no longer either a queen or a woman. [*Weeping and laughing.*] I'm like a terrified animal running this way and that. Argia: I've had a baby too, up in the mountains. You're the first person I've ever told.

ARGIA: Is that why you're going? You want to see the baby again?

THE QUEEN: Oh no! No! No! Why should I want to see him? Why should I love him? No, no, he only pursues me like all the rest. I'm running away from him as well. I don't want to see him. He can only be another threat to me. Let him stay where he is, and grow up in peace. [*She bursts into sobs.*] And may God forgive all of us.

ARGIA: Don't shake like that, my dear. Try and be calm. You'll be all right.

THE QUEEN [*whispering and laughing*]: Argia, I even think I'm . . . pregnant again. I keep feeling so hungry the whole time.

ARGIA [*looks at her, and gently strokes her face*]: You're covered in sweat. Wipe your face.

[*The hoot of an owl is heard outside.*]

THE QUEEN [*starting*]: That's the signal, isn't it? And now I have to go.

ARGIA: Wait a moment.

[*The signal is heard again.*]

THE QUEEN: Yes, it's the signal. Good-bye, Argia. Let me kiss you. [*She kisses* ARGIA *and gets ready to go to the door.*]

ARGIA: Wait.

THE QUEEN: Why do you say wait?

ARGIA: I didn't explain properly. That's not the way you must go out. They'll shoot you, if you go through that door.

THE QUEEN: What then?

ARGIA: It's through this other door. You must go through here. I've thought of a better plan.

THE QUEEN: How?

ARGIA: I'll push the door open on this side . . . oh, there won't be any danger. All I'll have to do is to push the door; they're such fools, they'll fire at once. The men on guard over that side will run round as soon as they hear the noise. That other door will be unprotected. You must seize the moment, and get away.

THE QUEEN: Shall I find the man there – the man who's to go with me?

ARGIA: No. Make for the mountains by yourself. You were probably right, it's safer that way.

[*The signal is heard again.*]

ARGIA [*pointing*]: Stand ready, over there. Quietly.

[*The* QUEEN *fumbles for a moment, and gives* ARGIA *a ring.*]

THE QUEEN: This was the last burden I had . . .

ARGIA [*putting it on*]: It's tight on me. So I shan't lose it.

[*The* QUEEN *goes and stands ready near one of the doors.* ARGIA *puts out the lamp; takes a pole, makes a sign of encouragement to the* QUEEN, *and goes cautiously over to the other door. She moves the door with the pole, and suddenly throws it wide open. A deafening burst of machine-gun fire splinters the door.* ARGIA *laughs silently. She makes a sign to the* QUEEN.]

ARGIA: Now! Go . . . Good-bye.

[*The* QUEEN *slips out.* ARGIA *stands waiting.*]

VOICES [*outside*]: On guard! On guard, there! Look out!

MAUPA [*coming in with his gun in his hands: to* ARGIA]: Don't you move!

ARGIA: You're irresistible.

MAUPA: And don't speak.

ARGIA: Oh, I wouldn't know what to say to you, anyway.

VOICES [*distant*]: On guard! On guard!

ANOTHER VOICE: On guard!

RAIM [*enters breathlessly*]: What's the matter?

MAUPA: This woman was trying to escape.

RAIM: My dear fellow . . . haven't you made a mistake?

MAUPA: I tell you she tried to get away! Perhaps you doubt my word?

RAIM: No, no. I'm sure you're right.

MAUPA: You watch her. I'll go and call the others. [*He goes out.*]

RAIM [*greatly agitated*]: What's happened? Where is she?

ARGIA: Gone.

RAIM: What have you done, you fool? And what are you going to tell them now?

ARGIA: I shall think up something; don't worry.

RAIM: Just you see you don't bring me into it . . . You needn't count on me . . . You'll get yourself out of it, I don't doubt . . . [*He breaks off at the sound of footsteps; turns to the newcomers; and says with emphasis*] Sir, this woman was trying to run away.

AMOS [*has entered, followed by* MAUPA. *He turns quietly to him*]: Friend, will you please point that gun downwards? We've no need of it. [MAUPA *does so.*]

AMOS [*to* RAIM]: And you, will you give the lady a seat? [RAIM *does so.*]

AMOS [*politely to* ARGIA]: Will you please sit down, madam? You wanted to go out?

ARGIA: I was thirsty.

AMOS: Ah, that explains it. You'll forgive us. At all events the incident has one good side to it. It offers us [*he points to* BIANTE, *who is coming in supported by the* PORTER] an opportunity of asking you to be good enough to grant us an interview . . . which I hope will be quiet and friendly. It's an opportunity I was looking for during the whole of our journey.

BIANTE [*coming forward and shouting*]: Light! Light! We might as well be in a cave! Bring some candles and lamps! Give us some illumination worthy of our cause.

[RAIM, MAUPA, *and the* PORTER *have already rushed out to fetch lights from the neighbouring rooms. The first to return is the* PORTER, *with a strong lamp. Its light falls on* ARGIA. *There is a moment of curious silence.*]

AMOS [*to* ARGIA]: Madam: what is your name?

CURTAIN

ACT THREE

Only a few seconds have gone by. RAIM, MAUPA, *and the* PORTER *are still bringing in lamps, and arranging the room. Then they all sit.* ARGIA *is standing in the midst of them.*

AMOS: Well?

ARGIA [*with hostile indifference*]: You will find my name, and everything else about me, in my documents. I have already been questioned once this evening, with the other travellers. Is this extra honour reserved for me alone?

AMOS: Madam: we have to ask you for a little further information.

ARGIA: There is no need to address me as madam. I'm only one of those very common plants you naturally find growing on the manure-heap of three wars.

AMOS: What is your nationality?

ARGIA: I was born in this country. And from that day to this, people like you have done nothing but repatriate me, expel me, deport me, search me, give me notice to quit; and so forth.

AMOS [*coldly polite*]: You sound as though you considered *us* responsible for all that.

ARGIA: Well, what are you doing now, if not giving orders? There are a great number of people in the world who've made it their job to decide what the rest of us have to do. Congratulations. You might tell me what it feels like.

AMOS: Have you never known what it feels like?

ARGIA: I? [*She pauses a moment, surprised.*] I? [*With a shrug.*] I've always been one of the people who take orders, not give them. It's my job to be here submitting to them, at this time of night; when I'm dropping with fatigue.

AMOS: Political necessities.

ARGIA: Ah, yes, political necessities: they're the reason we're forbidden to eat what we choose, every other day; the reason we're forbidden to go to bed when we're tired, or to light the fire when we're cold. 'Every time is the decisive time.' And how brazen you all are about it! It's been going on since Adam. Political necessities.

AMOS: Have you never used those words on your own behalf?

ARGIA [*surprised*]: I? My dear friend – you will forgive the expression – I've already told you that I've never done anything very useful or respectable in the whole of my life. Satisfied?

AMOS: What occupations have you followed up till now?

ARGIA: Oh, various ones. What I could pick up. You, and others like you, have always been so busy shouting that I've never had much chance to think about my own condition. There have been times when I've not been sorry if I could find someone willing to pay for my lunch or my dinner.

AMOS: Can you prove that?

ARGIA: Witnesses? Certainly, darling, certainly. Lots of men know me. I can prove it whenever I like.

BIANTE [*sneering: his voice is like a death-rattle*]: Have you any distinguishing marks on your body to prove your identity? Little things . . . that might have struck the attention of the men who paid for your lunches and dinners?

ARGIA [*after a pause; in a low voice*]: Yes. Men like you, and men even more repellent than you, if possible, have seen me and made use of me. That is what I am.

AMOS [*quieting* BIANTE *with a gesture*]: You don't seem to like us very much. Is there any special reason for that?

ARGIA: Yes: I always dislike the authorities: people who walk over our faces the whole time; and have rather a heavy tread.

AMOS [*still politely*]: Madam: I should perhaps convey to you some idea of the impression you are creating.

ARGIA: Well?

AMOS: The sharpness of your answers is in rather striking contrast with the humble condition you declare yourself to be in. And the bluntness you attempt to give those answers is in equally striking contrast with your obvious refinement and breeding.

ARGIA [*after a pause*]: Refinement and breeding? In me? You think I look . . . ? [*She laughs.*] How nice. You're trying to make love to me.

AMOS: I also have the impression that the liveliness of your behaviour is largely due to your need to conceal a certain amount of fear.

ARGIA: Fear? I?

AMOS: Yes.

ARGIA: Fear of whom? Of you? I realize that the contempt people feel for you makes you try and console yourselves with the idea that everyone's frightened of you. But I'm not frightened of you; why should I be? I've told you what I am. And I can prove it, whenever I choose.

BIANTE: Why not now?

ARGIA: Because, just at the moment, I happen to be enjoying myself. Yes, it's odd, isn't it? I'm actually enjoying myself.

BIANTE: Let's hope you go on enjoying yourself.

AMOS [*imperturbably*]: If your insolence fails to conceal your fear, your fear seems to be equally unsuccessful in curbing your insolence.

ARGIA [*ironically*]: I wonder why?

AMOS: Pride.

ARGIA: You think I'm proud, do you?

AMOS: Yes: with a pride which won't even listen to your own common sense when it warns you. You are scarcely even taking the trouble to lie successfully. What you would really like at this moment is to tell us you despise us.

ARGIA [*taking out a cigarette*]: As a matter of fact, it does strike me as slightly unnatural that people like you should give yourselves airs.

BIANTE: You'd better be careful, my dear; he was trained for the priesthood.

AMOS: An ancient pride which has soaked right through to your veins. Footsteps, used to the echo of surroundings where the press of the crowd is unknown. Hands, accustomed always to holding bright and precious objects; a voice that never had any need to raise itself in order to call for silence.

ARGIA [*after a moment's reflection*]: And that's what your intuition tells you about me, is it? All that?

AMOS: Madam, you are doing yourself a great deal of harm by lying to us. Suppose you come down to earth? Where were you born?

ARGIA [*is silent for a moment; then she laughs, and shrugging her shoulders, says with insulting sarcasm*]: I was born in one of the finest mansions in the city. I won't say whether it was on the first floor, or in the porter's lodge. In my room, when I woke, I always saw nymphs on the walls. The tapestries had hung there for five hundred years. Yes, you are right: I did, indeed, grow up among people who were silent the minute I indicated that I was about to speak. And when they answered me, it was always in pleasant voices, saying pleasant things. [*Mockingly.*] I walked on carpets as large as a village square! The doors were always opened for me! The rooms were always heated: I have always been sensitive to the cold. The food was excellent; I have always been rather greedy. My dear friend, you should have seen the tablecloths, and the silver! The crystal goblets I used to drink from!

AMOS: And all this good fortune cost *you* very little trouble.

ARGIA [*in satirically affected tones*]: We don't ask the rose what trouble it has taken: we ask it simply to be a rose: and to be as different as it can from an artichoke. They used to bring me whatever I wanted on beautiful carved trays; then they would bow and retire, always turning at the door and bowing once again before they went out. [*Indicating her cigarette.*] Do you mind?

AMOS [*going across and lighting it*]: And why did you insist on their doing all that?

ARGIA: I didn't insist. They wanted to. And you know, I think you too, if I were to smile at you, would also wag your tails. But no, the price would be too high: for me, I mean. Your arrogance is simply your way of bolstering yourselves up. And I . . . [*She breaks off.*]

AMOS [*in lighting the cigarette, has noticed the ring*]: That's a very beautiful ring you have there.

ARGIA [*tries to remove it, but cannot*]: It won't come off. [*Lightly.*] I've been wearing it too long. It's a family heirloom. [*She looks for a moment at them all; then laughs, with mocking bitterness.*] Yes; in my time, I've been a proud woman . . . rich . . . highly respected, elegant, happy . . . fortunate . . .

AMOS [*coldly*]: And your political opinions?

ARGIA: I'm not interested in politics.

AMOS: But at least you prefer one party to the other!

ARGIA: Do you?

AMOS: Yes.

ARGIA: Then I prefer the opposite one.

AMOS: Why?

ARGIA: For the simple reason that I don't like the way you behave. You strut about a great deal too much. [*With derisive affectation.*]

You see, ever since I was a child I have been brought up to respect people of a very different sort from you. People who washed properly, and wore clean-smelling linen. Perhaps there's some political significance in that! I can't believe that an unpleasant smell gives people special rights. Or perhaps the revolution has a smell!

BIANTE: The smell of bitter soup in the people's tenements.

ARGIA [*affectedly*]: I'm sorry. I have never smelt it. I think you probably give yourselves too much work to do; you smell of sweat.

AMOS: The stonebreakers and the poor who follow us have less delicate nostrils.

ARGIA: That must be very sad for them.

BIANTE [*with painful vehemence*]: Tomorrow we shall have no stonebreakers and no poor!

ARGIA [*insolently*]: We shall have other troubles. Otherwise what would *you* do? You canalize people's miseries. You turn them first into envy, then into fury. The thick rind of bad temper on the world has grown a great deal thicker since you began to cultivate it. The number of the dead has grown too. And all your great ideas don't prevent a distinct smell of blood rising from you.

BIANTE: Amos, for God's sake!

AMOS [*cutting him short*]: Do you realize where all these questions are leading?

ARGIA: Yes.

AMOS: Is there anyone here who can identify you?

ARGIA: Certainly. Otherwise I would hardly be taking such risks.

AMOS: Who is it?

ARGIA: I'll tell you later. The night is long ... and so is the mountain-road. Provided *you* have the time to spare ...

[*A* SOLDIER *has entered, and has whispered something into* BIANTE'S *ear.*]

ARGIA: .... though they do say that gun-fire can be heard round about. Bad news? Is that what's worrying you?

AMOS: Don't hope for miracles; they don't happen any more.

BIANTE: Stop it, Amos, make her talk, for God's sake! Make her talk, I'm in a hurry! My body's burning as if it would set the whole bloody world on fire.

ARGIA [*insolently*]: Moderate your voice, please. [*Suddenly and passionately.*] If I were the Queen ... If I were the Queen, do you know what I would say to you at this moment? [*In a manner not devoid of majesty.*] I'd say: 'Gentlemen.' [*She drops into a more normal tone, but soon returns to her former manner.*] 'Gentlemen, you are angry with me; but I am not angry with you. Neither the power you have usurped, nor your threats, are capable of disturbing me. We are far apart. It is that that makes you boil with rage; and keeps me calm.'

AMOS: If you're not the Queen, I'm bound to say you give a very good imitation of the haughty way in which she'd behave on an occasion like this.

ARGIA: The reason is that I've been rehearsing this role for a very long time. Every time any one has been rude to me – and that can happen to anyone, can't it? – every time I've come away with my cheeks still burning, what scathing retorts, what tremendous, noble answers I've always imagined! I know everything a woman of spirit can say to put the insolent in their places . . .

[*The noise of hoarse voices begins to be heard outside.*]

ARGIA [*continues passionately*]: And if I were the Queen I'd say to you: 'It's true, gentlemen, there was no mob round me, there was space. The echo used to carry my words on high and purify them . . . make them lonely; and calm. The echo used to liberate them . . . [*Slightly intoxicated by her own words, she plays with the echo.*] Re . . . gi . . . na . . . It made them mount upward . . . up . . . on high . . . high . . . high . . . it wanted them to be calm and just . . . Re . . . gi . . . na . . .'

[*They have all, one after another, stood up; they stand listening to that echo, and to the distant voices.*]

BIANTE [*suddenly*]: What's happening? What's the matter, out there? Who are those people coming up the road? Why are we wasting time? My fever's getting worse; I'm burning all over. What are our weapons for? Yes, we do need dead people! What are we waiting for? Are you waiting till I'm dead here in the middle of them? [*To the* PORTER.] What's going on out there?

THE PORTER [*has been out: and now re-enters, distressed*]: General and Commissar Amos! Something's happening. The road out there is black with people.

BIANTE: Who are they?

THE PORTER: The people living in the upper valley. They must have got to hear about this woman, they must have heard she'd been caught, and they've come down under cover of the dark.

ARGIA: I told you, did I not, that your power was only provisional?
[BIANTE *is already hobbling quickly out.* AMOS, RAIM, *and* MAUPA *follow him.*]

THE PORTER [*remains alone with* ARGIA. *He looks at her; and suddenly, with impulsive reverence, takes off his cap; he is at once ashamed of himself, and pretends to be looking at a sheet of paper on the table beside him. As though reading from the paper; in a low voice*]: There are a great many cowards in this world, who are so frightened that they hide their true feelings; and I am the lowest and most cowardly of them all. But for us, more than for others, what comfort and healing it brings, to know that there is someone . . . [*his eyes do not move from the sheet of paper, but his voice rises slightly*] . . . there is someone who is still unafraid, and can stand alone against all the rest! What consolation, for us in our shame, to think that in a soul shaped like our own, everything that in us is ruined, stays faithful and untarnished! To know that such a creature has drawn breath in this world! I believe that even God Himself, hearing her speak, is proud of her. And whoever shall think of her, though it be a thousand years from now, shall feel once more upon his face a look of dignity. [*His voice has become louder, but his eyes have never once raised themselves from the sheet of paper.*]

[MAUPA *and* RAIM *come in, holding the door open for* BIANTE.]

BIANTE [*goes up to* ARGIA, *and suddenly bursts into a laugh*]: Hahaha! Your majesty! Yes, your famous name has brought a lot of people down from the mountains to meet you. Do you know what sort of help they're bringing you? Do you know what they want? [*Almost casually.*] To see you condemned to death and hanged.

MAUPA [*with quiet ecstasy*]: We want to see the colour of the Queen's entrails.

AMOS [*entering and raising his hand*]: There will be a proper trial. Otherwise we should be showing very little trust in our own purpose.

BIANTE [*shouting*]: Proper trial! Formal procedure! To hell with this chattering. I've no time to waste. I can't feel my own hands any more; I can hardly keep my eyes open.

AMOS: A jury will sit. [*To* MAUPA.] You: Go and bring some of those people in here.

BIANTE [*to* MAUPA, *as he goes out*]: And choose people who look sensible, and keep their eyes on the ground!

AMOS: Peasants merely: but now they have authority: optimists, and the world is full of them; in revolutions they are manna dropped from heaven. Every one of them believes that the sickle will cut the whole meadow but will stop a quarter of an inch short of his own throat.

BIANTE: And the jury ought to have a few beggars on it as well . . .

AMOS: . . . a few people who are stupid and lazy, and imagine that a change in the insignia over the doors will give them the reward of the industrious and the intelligent . . .

[*A number of peasants, men and women, have entered. The* ENGINEER *is among them.*]

BIANTE [*to the newcomers*]: Come in, my friends! Sit down. You already know that I have taken over the command. That means that everybody can kill a man, but I can do it with a roll of drums like an acrobat making a difficult leap. The republic has conquered. [*He beats his fist on the table.*] Well, then I preside! [*To* AMOS.] You shall be the accuser! [*To* RAIM.] You shall write. [*To the newcomers.*] You shall judge! [*Lowering his voice.*] And after that, I, as president, if I'm still alive, shall carry out the sentence. You can begin, Amos.

[AMOS *has already risen: he speaks in the tones of a chancellor reading out an act.*]

AMOS: The accusation charges this woman with having concealed her identity, and falsified her papers.

ARGIA: Gentlemen! Please, please listen to me. I came up here . . .

AMOS: . . . with the intention of fleeing the country? Or to try to discover the whereabouts of your son? Yes, madam, we are fully informed about that also. Your son. [*His voice slightly rising.*] She is also accused of having formerly exercised a secret and illicit influence on the heads of the state, inducing them to enact factious and oppressive laws . . .

BIANTE: Oh, get on with it, Amos! You're cold, you've got no guts! You're just being cruel!

AMOS [*louder*]: . . . of inciting to massacre and persecution . . .

ARGIA: But I have never done anything of the kind!

AMOS: . . . of having fomented conspiracies aimed at undermining the authority of the State . . .

ARGIA: But that's what you've done! And you blame it on the Queen! *You* were the sowers of discord.

AMOS [*louder*]: . . . to the point of inducing a number of fanatics to take up arms against their country.

ARGIA: But I . . .

AMOS: This woman is accused of having herself unloosed the present conflict; of having herself driven it to atrocious excesses. She herself summoned to this country foreign armed forces, herself lit the fires that now smoke from every point of the horizon, herself disfigured the dead along the roads . . .

ARGIA: But I tell you I . . .

AMOS: . . . didn't know? Didn't want it?

ARGIA: I tell you that my hands . . .

AMOS: Are clean? Is that it? That only shows how cunning you've been. It deprives you of extenuating circumstances, if there ever were any.

THE ENGINEER [*suddenly and violently*]: I was walking in the street one day: there was a cordon of soldiers; and they said to me: 'Not this way, the Queen will be coming down here.' I went round another way, and they told me: 'You can't come through here.' Everywhere I went, it was the same. Madam, you were always in the way.

ARGIA: Friends, friends, but I was there too, with you; on your side of the cordon, not the other.

A PEASANT-WOMAN [*suddenly bursting into sobs*]: The shirt I washed for my son, he said it was shabby. He said the soup I cooked for him tasted nasty. And now they've told me that he's lying out there, in the fields, with his arms wide open, covered with ants. It's all the Queen's fault.

ARGIA: You stone that woman now, only because you one day fawned on her!

A PEASANT [*violently*]: When our children are old enough to play games, they're not allowed to play the same games as rich men's children. That's a terrible thing! That's what poisons their minds!

THE PEASANT-WOMAN: My son hated the earthen crockery, he hated the smell of our home; he hated his own life!

THE PEASANT: My daughter went away with the soldiers, and I haven't heard a word of her since. That was your fault!

THE WOMAN: It was your fault!

BIANTE: All of you! All of you! Bear witness, all of you!

THE ENGINEER: It was her fault!

MAUPA: It was her fault!

OTHERS: Her fault! It was her fault!

BIANTE: And what about you? That porter over there! Are you the only one with nothing to say?

    [*A silence.*]

THE PORTER: Yes ... everything she did ... humiliated us.

ARGIA [*rebelliously, to the* PORTER]: And who was it who taught you humiliation and envy? Who was it who let your rancour loose?

AMOS [*with sudden intensity*]: You, the apex of privilege, the symbol of prerogative; you, the emblem of those distinctions from which humiliation and rivalry were born. Your whole authority is based and built upon inequality. It is in you that injustice is personified, it is in you she finds her arrogant features, her scornful voice, her contemptuous answers, her sumptuous clothes, and her unsoiled hands. Your name of Queen is of itself enough to make men see that they are unequal: on one side vast revenues, on the other, vast burdens. You are the hook from which the great act of tyranny hangs. The world will be a less unhappy place when you have vanished from it.

ARGIA [*remains for a long moment with her head bent*]: Forgive me. I have been play-acting a little: perhaps too much. Now I will tell you the truth. I can prove that I am not the Queen, and I can prove it at once. There is someone here who can witness for me.

BIANTE: Who is it?

ARGIA: That man over there, your interpreter. Stop, Raim, don't run away. He knows me only too well. He knows I'm not a queen. I'm the sort of woman who has to smile at lodging-house keepers, and traffic in pawn-tickets.

RAIM [*comes forward slowly, in silence*]: There must be some misunderstanding. This woman must be mad. I've never seen her before in my life.

ARGIA: Look at me, Raim.

RAIM: I am looking at you. [*To* AMOS.] I've never seen her before.

ARGIA [*turning to the others*]: My friend is frightened things may have gone too far. Whether I'm the Queen or not, or he's my friend or not, he's afraid you just have to have a certain number of people to shoot up here. He just wants to stay alive, that's all.

RAIM: I knew you'd say that. But I must insist that I do not know you.

ARGIA: Gentlemen! I and this man, who 'doesn't know' me, kept each other warm all through one whole winter!

RAIM: Rubbish!

ARGIA: I came up here solely to look for him. There are people here who saw us talking.

RAIM [to the others]: Of course they did. I tried to approach her: because I thought she looked suspicious. I don't know who she is. I'm sorry, madam, but I can't help you.

[He moves away, disappearing among the others. ARGIA stands for a moment in silence.]

ARGIA [almost absently]: Perhaps it's true. Perhaps that man and I never did know one another. But, even so, gentlemen, that doesn't give you the right to make stupid mistakes. If you have to have a corpse to show people, when you tell them the Queen's dead, you might at least look for a corpse a bit more like her. You fools! I, the Queen? Is mine the voice of a queen . . .? Has my life been the life of a queen . . .? [Suddenly calling.] Raim! Raim! Call him back!

AMOS: I'd like to bet that your friend is far away by now; and making for the mountains like a hare.

ARGIA [bewildered]: Gentlemen, there is someone else who can witness for me. There were two women travellers in this room. I . . . and another woman.

AMOS [amiably]: Yes. [He makes a sign to one of the soldiers, who at once goes out.]

ARGIA: . . . a peasant-woman.

AMOS [amiably]: Yes, And where is she now?

ARGIA: She ran away. But she can't be far off. That woman . . . can tell you . . . that I'm not what you think. And you will have what you want, just the same. Send out and look for her.

AMOS: Up in the mountains?

ARGIA: Yes.

AMOS: All you can say of your witnesses, is that one is fleeing and the other has fled. [A pause.] Madam, we have a surprise for you. [A pause.] Your peasant-woman is here. She didn't get very far. Here she is.

[In a great silence the QUEEN appears, escorted by the soldier. The QUEEN, pale, and rather stiff, looks round her. AMOS points to ARGIA.

The QUEEN *comes forward to* ARGIA; *and speaks to her with a slight stammer.*]

THE QUEEN: Forgive me, my dear . . . it was all no use . . . I knew they'd have caught me . . . The moment I was so frightened of . . . arrived . . . But I don't think . . . they've caught me in time . . . to hurt me. I managed to fool them . . . you know how . . . I prefer it . . . to be all over at once. Good-bye, my dearest friend. I was so afraid . . . but not so much, now. [*She sways, and sinks slowly to the ground.*]

BIANTE: What's the matter?

ARGIA [*kneels down beside the* QUEEN, *and takes her hand. After a while she looks up, and says, as though lost in thought*] : She carried poison with her. [*A pause.*] You have killed her.

AMOS [*cutting her short*] : You are now completely without accomplices. Say something, why don't you?

BIANTE [*shouting*] : You've no one left now!

AMOS: It's all over with you, your majesty! Answer us! You are the Queen!

ARGIA [*rises slowly*] : Not every eye shall look to the ground. There shall still be someone to stand before you. Yes. I am the Queen! [*A silence.*]

BIANTE: She's confessed, Amos. Quick, make your speech for the prosecution.

AMOS [*rises, and thinks for a moment*] : If friction is to be stopped, the only way is to remove the cause; if disturbances are to be brought to an end, the only way is to eliminate the disturber. I see only one way to make such eliminations final.

[*The witnesses, perturbed by the decision by which they are to be faced, rise cautiously, first one, then another, trying to efface themselves.*]

AMOS: No other method is known whereby revolutions may be at once prudent and rapid; nor any other argument that makes them so persuasive; nor any procedure which more effectively seals dangerous lips and more finally immobilizes enemy hands.

[*The witnesses have cautiously moved towards the door, but at this point* AMOS'S *look arrests them.*]

AMOS [*continuing*] : Such a method serves also, among other things, to identify the weak pillars; in fact, you will notice that some of our jurymen who have divined the responsibility that is about to face them, are cautiously trying to slip away one by one: they do not realize that, in the course of time, that may render them also liable to furnish proofs of the excellence of the method. It is quite true the importance of a revolution is in proportion to the number of dead it produces. Biante, it is your duty to pronounce sentence.

BIANTE [*exhausted and swaying, rises, supported by* MAUPA] : The revolution has decided that the Queen must die. I order . . . I order . . . [*He cannot go on, he has come to the end.* MAUPA *lifts him back into his chair.*]

AMOS: You are no longer in a position to give orders. Your post is vacant. [*He turns to the others.*] The revolution has decided that the Queen must die. The sentence will be carried out during the course of the night.

CURTAIN

ACT FOUR

A short time has elapsed since the previous act. ARGIA *is dozing. In the background, a soldier is asleep on a wooden chair.* AMOS *comes in: he shakes the soldier, and sends him away. Then he wakes* ARGIA.

AMOS: I've come to inform you that the sentence must be carried out very shortly. The messenger who is to take the news of the execution to my government must leave during the night. In fact, we all have to leave this area before morning, for unexpected military reasons.

ARGIA [*half-absently*]: Yes.

AMOS: I also have to tell you that you can discount any possibility of rescue. Any move on the part of the Coalitionists would be ineffective: arrangements have already been made to carry out the sentence at the first alarm.

ARGIA: Was this the only reason you came to see me?

AMOS: No. On the contrary. There is a much more important reason. In fact, you may regard everything that has happened so far tonight as a mere preamble to what I have to tell you now.

ARGIA: Well?

AMOS: Do you really think the revolution would have given so much of its time to your frivolities this evening, and taken so much trouble to give an appearance of legality to the trial, if we had no precise aim in mind?

ARGIA: Well, what is it?

AMOS: The revolution intends to be irreproachable right to the end. I have come to tell you that you are free to ask for pardon.

ARGIA: From whom?

AMOS: From us. Will you ask for it?

ARGIA [*after a pause*]: I will ask for it.

AMOS: Good. The coldness of the night seems to have brought you to your senses. [*He sits.*] Naturally the pardon is dependent on certain conditions.

ARGIA: What are they?

AMOS: Formal ones. Futile even. Before I disclose them to you, I would like you to realize exactly what would happen to you in the event of the pardon being refused. The human mind often seeks refuge in vagueness. However: outside this building is a stone platform. On it, when you went out, you would see six armed soldiers. You would then go and stand in front of them. You would fall. A short while after, the sunrise would illuminate a universe in all respects as usual, except that you would not be there. That is all.

ARGIA: The conditions.

AMOS: The signing of a list of declarations concerning the events of the last few years. The witnesses are ready. [He turns to the door.] Come in.

[The PORTER and MAUPA come in and remain in the background.]

ARGIA: What sort of declarations?

AMOS: Saying that you acknowledge that you have conspired, et cetera, have summoned foreign help against your country, et cetera, and confess yourself guilty of illegal actions, dishonourable conduct, et cetera.

ARGIA [almost indifferently]: They sound like lies to me.

AMOS: You will also be required to give us certain information. But that we can go into later.

ARGIA: Is the paper ready?

AMOS: Here it is.

[He makes a sign, and the PORTER approaches ARGIA with a paper in his hand. She turns, and sees him; she has stretched out her hand; now she withdraws it. The PORTER puts the paper in her hand.]

AMOS: I forgot to give you one other piece of news. The flight of your accomplice – the so-called interpreter, I mean – was unsuccessful. They had to fire at him; I am afraid he was seriously wounded. In the hope of surviving and winning our clemency, he employed his last moments in betraying you even more comprehensively than he had done before. He confirmed all the allegations made in that document.

ARGIA [thoughtfully]: Poor Raim. His eyes were a nice colour; it was pleasant to look into them. How terribly concerned he was to keep them open on the world. In vain, apparently. Good-bye, Raim. This wind is carrying all the leaves away.

AMOS: Yes, madam. It's the time of year. Whole gatherings of people who yesterday sat in gilded halls, could today reassemble in hell with no one missing. Your other accomplice, the peasant-woman, was at least able to say good-bye to you.

ARGIA [*thoughtfully*]: She was so terrified; so very unpractical. She wanted to sleep, night after night, in peace. Good-bye.

AMOS: I mean that you are now alone. But alive, luckily for you. Try and remain so. In times like these, and at so small a cost [*pointing to the paper*], it's a good bargain.

ARGIA: To tell you the truth, I scarcely know any longer whether I want to make a good bargain or not. [*She takes an uncertain step forward; sees the* PORTER *staring at her; and stands still again.*] But, Commissar Amos, you must really think me very simple, if you imagine you can deceive me so easily. No, I know as well as you do that there is no way out of this. [*She gives back the paper to* AMOS.] To survive and to be able to describe such things would be hard enough even for your witnesses. And think who the chief character is. No. It wouldn't be a very clever move on your part to allow the Queen to go free, so that the common people could come and kiss the hem of her garments while she described to them how you forced her signature from her.

AMOS: A reasonable objection. We had thought of it already. It also explains your courage earlier this evening . . . [*with a faint suggestion of bitterness*] a courage which would have been a very humiliating slap in the face for us, if we hadn't been aware how gratuitous and false and easy it was: as courage usually is, in my opinion. Madam: you thought then that everything was lost already; so your fine gestures cost you nothing. Very well, I've come to tell you that in fact nothing is lost, so far as you're concerned. The revolution has an interest in keeping you alive. [*A pause.*] Alive, and in circulation. Alive . . . [*almost casually*] and in disgrace. Confess. And first you'll be despised; then ignored. And then: no longer a queen, but a woman: a woman, no longer walking on fine soft carpets, but huddled on the hard floor of an all-night bar, learning the pleading smiles of poverty . . .

ARGIA [*lost in her recollections*]: . . . listening to the cheap jokes of the barman, with an anxious smile on her face; soothing and flattering the bad-tempered taxi-driver . . . [*The eye of the* PORTER *is on her.*]

But who, who on earth, could ever conceive that a woman of such birth and spirit, stainless and honourable, could foul herself by signing such a document? They'll never be willing to believe that.

AMOS: They will have to believe it. We shall give them the proof. I've already told you that you will furnish us with certain information, information you alone possess. On that information we shall act. And the world will be compelled to realize that it was you who gave it to us.

ARGIA [*with melancholy indifference*]: . . . And so . . . poor Queen in disgrace . . . you spare her, and the others cut her throat; her friends.

AMOS: At least it would be time gained. Unless – and this is the point – some of the others, your friends, I mean . . . [*Breaking off: to* MAUPA.] You go outside.

[MAUPA *goes out.*]

AMOS [*to the* PORTER]: You wait over there. [*He turns back to* ARGIA.] I was speaking about the others, your friends: in order that we can take steps to protect you and save you from them [*dropping his voice*] you will tell us their names. [*With a sudden cry, pointing a finger at her.*] Yes! You know them! I saw it! I read it there, in your eyes! They glinted. You've seen the way to save yourself. And you know you have it there at your disposal: inside your head. [*Persuasively.*] Well, then, first: it's clearly in the interest of the revolution to keep you alive so that respect for you shall die out. Secondly: it's indispensable that the revolution shall know the names of your accomplices. The two things fit together; and save you. Your disclosures will be the beginning of a great clean-up. There are cold-blooded vipers lying curled up in our very beds. Illustrious personages and obscure imbeciles. Even here, a short time ago; it was quite clear that your fine speeches were directed to someone's ears. They will all be rendered permanently harmless. [*His voice drops to a whisper.*] Who are they? Where are they? What are their names? Quickly: tell me their names.

ARGIA [*stands for a moment with bent head*]: Your voice went very quiet when you asked me for them, didn't it? If it made you feel sick to ask for them, what do you suppose I should feel if I were to divulge them? [*With a wan smile.*] It's obviously not a thing to be very proud of. And unfortunately, I don't know any names.

AMOS: You not only know them: you've already wisely decided to disclose them to me. However, you will no doubt make me wait a little for them; that was to be expected, and I shall not refuse to indulge you. It's a due one has to pay to the concept of honour. You merely want to be persuaded.

ARGIA [*with a wan smile*]: The men you want me to hand over to you certainly never expected this as their reward.

AMOS: Those men have simply staked everything on one card. In their complete selfishness, they were prepared to make use of you. Do you know any of them personally; or feel affection for any of them? No. Bonds of gratitude? No. [*Ironically.*] Is it for some political idea that you are prepared to sacrifice yourself?

ARGIA [*almost absently*]: I know very little about such things; I've told you that before.

AMOS: Or perhaps the thought of your good name is holding you back? The little plaster figure of your reputation crashing in pieces? Madam: don't take any notice of cant-phrases; follow nature: which fears death, and knows nothing else. Only thus will you be sincere, and therefore honourable. After all, the finest reputation in the world is very little comfort to a corpse.

ARGIA [*thoughtfully*]: Yes.

AMOS: Good. [*Although the room is almost empty, and the silence in it is absolute.*] Well, then, gentlemen, silence! The Queen is deciding. [*A silence.*]

ARGIA: So my decisions can actually make people hold their breath. Messengers are getting ready to announce them beyond the mountains.

AMOS: That does not, however, give you one minute's extra time. [*He calls.*] Maupa!

MAUPA [*appearing in the doorway*]: Everything is ready.

AMOS [*dismissing him with a wave*]: Good. Tell them to wait.

ARGIA: I am a person who can make people wait. It's the first time that's ever happened to me. I can say yes: I can say no.

AMOS: You have very little time left, madam.

ARGIA: Do not try to hurry the Queen. The Queen. I am only just beginning to realize what it means to be one.

AMOS: It means obeying a few flatterers in order to rule over many subjects.

ARGIA: Not at all. To be a queen really means: to be alone. It means:

to have gone on ahead, to have left everyone else behind. Enemies, friends: all gone. A great simplicity. This room is indeed a palace; your aversion from me is only a form of respect; you are only a rebel subject. I can say yes; I can say no.

AMOS: At a price, however.

ARGIA: It is the only one I can pay. [*She suddenly shivers with cold.*] And suppose I decide to pay it? I am free: to say yes, or no. And no one in the world can do anything about it. I am the one who decides. It's beautiful; to be able to talk to you like this; to look about me like this . . . and to feel my breathing so free, and the beating of my heart so peaceful.

[AMOS *has taken up the cloak left by the soldier, and places it round her shoulders.*]

AMOS: You are shivering.

ARGIA: It is the cold that announces the dawn. The only thing I am afraid of is getting tired; it's been a wearing night. [*A pause.*] I don't even feel dislike towards you.

AMOS: The technique of pride, is it not? The technique of pride. [*With sudden anger.*] But pride is not flesh and blood, madam! The chosen creature's superiority with which you think you can even now keep us at a distance! But it's not your flesh and blood! It's a shell! A crust, that's all. Born of habit. Like the hardness of the hands of a peasant. But you haven't earned it by digging. It's come to you from the bowings and scrapings of a whole palace all round you since the day you were born! Give me those names. Firmness, honour, eyes that never lower themselves, the technique of pride: I'd like to know what would be left of all that, if you'd had to live in some of the places I've known, and cooked yourself an egg over a spirit-lamp, and gone out of an evening in a greasy overcoat, with a nice smile ready to try and soften the man at the dairy. Yes, yes, our eyes can't look at people as yours do . . . even our thoughts, here inside us, are a bit grubby, and shabby, and common, and bruised by rubbing shoulders with the crowd . . . But don't try to imagine they are so very different from your own. Just lift the curtain a little. Come on, give me the names. If I were to twist your wrist, you'd scream like the rest of us! Your majesty, have you ever seen the little white grubs in rotten meat? They suddenly spurt out, and writhe about furiously. Minute as they are, they want to live;

to feed; to reproduce; they do exactly what we do; you: everyone: and in exactly the same way. The proud boast of being a person, a will, someone distinguished, is no more than a matter of fine linen. Take people's clothes away from them; and that's exactly what they'll be. All naked, equal grubs, wriggling about as best they can. The slightest planetary disturbance could quietly wipe everything out. And instead of wriggling as equals, do we have to give one man heaven and another man hell? Come down from your tin-pot throne. Get used to these things. Get used to being reasonable. Let your own instincts win; and be afraid: it's your way of wriggling. Give me those names.

ARGIA [her teeth chattering]: What you're saying, in fact, is that if there were here, in my place, some less fortunate woman than I, someone who'd had to cook herself an egg in her room, you're saying that there'd be some real merit in *her*, if she were courageous at this moment? Commissar Amos, there was once a woman whom they played a joke on. I was told about it. One Sunday, this woman went to the seaside. And the bathing-attendants, for a joke, knowing the sort of woman she was, got out for her a bathing-costume of the kind that becomes almost transparent in the water. There was a good deal of merriment. And all of a sudden, the woman noticed that everyone was looking at her, and that there was rather a row going on.

AMOS: Come on: the names.

ARGIA: And at last that woman saw that she was standing there almost naked! Alone and naked. She stood there bewildered. And suddenly, do you know what she did? She tried to laugh, with them. [*Controlling herself, and shrugging her shoulders.*] And after all, what did they see? That she was a woman. We know what a woman is. A man comes up to her . . . cheerful, with his big sweaty hands, and says: 'Do this . . . go like this . . . do that . . . [*louder*] . . . go on . . .' [*Suddenly, with a real cry of anguish and protest.*] Well, do you know what I think? I think there comes a time when the only thing to do is to stand up and say . . . [*as though actually turning on someone*] 'Why do you insult me like this? And, my God, why have I allowed you to? Get away from me! Go away! Go away! Leave me alone! You take advantage of an immense mistake, a monstrous delusion! Respect me! Show me respect! Respect . . . because I am

... the Queen! The Queen, and destined for other things than this.'
[*With a change of voice.*] What I want to do is to go out of doors, as
if it were a fine morning, and as if I had seen down there, at the end
of the street, the cool fresh colour of the sea, a colour that makes the
heart leap! And someone stops me, and then someone else, and
someone else, with the usual rudeness. But this morning I don't
even hear them. I'm not afraid any longer. My face expresses dignity. I am as I would always have wished to be. And it would have
been simple after all. It would have been enough to want to be.
Palaces have nothing to do with it. It was my own fault.

AMOS [*after a long pause*]: Am I to take this to mean that you still
refuse? [*Almost with melancholy.*] Very well; in that case, your
troubles are not yet over. Madam: you are forcing me to do this,
remember.

[*He goes to the door, and makes a sign to someone outside.* MAUPA
*enters slowly, leading by the hand a small boy about three years old,
dressed in peasant-boy's clothes.*]

AMOS: You can go, now, Maupa. So can you, porter.

[MAUPA *and the* PORTER *go out. The boy is left standing alone in the
middle of the room.*]

ARGIA [*shaken*]: Who is he?

AMOS [*with the same melancholy, moving to the child's side*]: It is the person who will persuade you.

ARGIA [*desperately*]: I don't know who he is!

AMOS: I know of course that you don't actually recognize him. We
ourselves had a great deal of trouble in tracing him.

ARGIA [*cries out*]: I swear to you! I swear ... that he isn't my son! I'm
not his mother!

AMOS: He's a fine child. He'll be able to live and grow up as an un-
knowing peasant ... so long as the protection you are according to
a few seditious men doesn't force us to eliminate in him any pretext
for sedition in the future. In such an orgy of blood, the scales won't
be upset by a few drops more ... Well, that is what you wanted:
to choose: now you can do so.

ARGIA [*instinctively clutching her face*]: He isn't mine! I tell you he isn't
mine.

AMOS: It is in your power to choose. The weight of this tiny little boy
puts an end to your flights of fancy, and brings you back to earth.

Even the wolves in the woods up here love their young. Yes: that's a real thing: the rest is smoke. Make your choice: make it according to nature: no one will condemn you.

ARGIA [*astounded*]: And if I don't, you're capable of a crime like this?

AMOS [*with lofty sadness*]: Madam: I shall do everything that is necessary. Common reproaches should be reserved for common occasions. The blood that your disclosures will make flow may be a great deal, but it will be far away. There is only a little here. But it is warm. And it is your own.

ARGIA: Oh God, how can a human mind have so much hate in it?

AMOS [*with painful intensity*]: It is not hate. But it is too late to argue now. I also made my choice once upon a time. However a stone rolls, the one who has dislodged it rolls down with it.

ARGIA: My God, how can you . . . break laws so sacred . . . ? I tell you he isn't mine! Did you keep me alive only to save me for this? I swear to you he isn't mine, take him away, take him away . . . Oh God, oh God, how can you think you've the power to . . . [*Crying out.*] In what name, by what right, do you dare to do this?

AMOS [*shouting her down*]: In what name! By what right! [*Suddenly controlling himself.*] Listen to me: I want to tell *you* something also. When we overthrew the October republic, I was in the palace too. An agreement had been reached; our victory was total and peaceful. There had been no bloodshed. All the same, we were in the palace rooms; we wanted to pull down the coats-of-arms. We began to unnail them. A man was fetching great blows at one of the trophies. And I noticed that little by little something seemed to dawn on his face. Down below in the street the crowds were yelling. Suddenly this man, as soon as he'd knocked the trophy off the wall, turned round. He was covered in sweat. And he hurled his axe at one of the mirrors! The others followed suit. Then they began to smash everything. And their faces were furious, they were intoxicated, they were beautiful, they were holy. The smoke was already appearing! And the fire followed! [*Controlling himself suddenly.*] But it would have been contemptible if the aim of all was merely to take a few pence from the hand of a fat dead man and put them in the hand of a thin living man. So much noise simply in order to modify a few tariffs and initiate a few austere apostles into the pleasures of wearing silk shirts? But this fury, which spouts up like a fountain of black oil, comes from deep down, madam, it's the distillation of a very different grief, the memory of a very different betrayal, it doesn't merely utter its 'no' to your silks and satins and the farmer's hoard. [*He cries.*] It says 'no' to everything there is! It says rage towards everything, despair towards everything! What we hear coming towards us down there, is the thunder of the great waterfall! It's towards the great rapids that the boat is rushing! This fury says 'no' to the whole world: it says [*with despairing weariness*] that the world is wrong, it's all absurdity; an immense, unchangeable quarry of despair, a grotesque, unchangeable labyrinth of injustice, an insensate clockwork, that one day compels you and me to say and do what we're saying and doing now. It says 'no'; total sterilization; away with everything: the just and the unjust, loyalty and betrayal, worthiness, guilt, glory [*he points to* ARGIA] ... everything that makes us grasping and boastful owners in life and in death, all this mass of falsehoods, this immense fraud! Tell me the names.

ARGIA [*staring at the child*]: The names? But you'll kill him whatever happens, I know you will. [*A brief pause.*] Oh, poor little child, in his little peasant's dress! No one wants him. His mother runs away from him. I've done nothing but say: 'Take him away.' Completely alone. [*She suddenly runs to the child, and hugs him tightly.*] Oh, what a lovely child you are, my darling. How healthy you are. And what pretty little teeth. My angel, your mother won't ever come and see if you're asleep, she'll never see you run, and say: 'Look how he's grown.' He isn't at all sleepy, is he, and not the tiniest bit afraid, is he? No, no, he's very well, he's in the warm ... [*She is pressing him against her breast.*] ... This is the right place for a little boy to be, isn't it? This is a little throne for a child ... [*She turns to* AMOS.] Sir, I've been deceiving myself. I thought that everything would be simple. Perhaps I should after all do as you say ... I ought to tell you those names ... I'm so confused ... Wait a moment ... those names ... [*She stands there, with eyes wide-open, looking before her; suddenly she laughs softly; and whispers.*] A miracle, sir. A miracle. I've forgotten them! Perhaps I have been too much upset, or perhaps I have been helped in some way; but that step has been spared me. [*She hugs the child tightly, hiding her face against him, and remains thus.*]

AMOS [*after a long pause*]: In that case the struggle between us is over. All that remains is to finish what was begun. [*A pause; then, seriously and gently.*] If you believe in the survival of your soul, and desire a confessor, anyone you choose may hear you.

ARGIA: Yes, I do desire it. [*She rises without letting go the child.*] I have made sad and improvident use of my person, my words, my thoughts, and for the most part, of the whole of my life. I laid the blame for this upon others, when the blame was all my own. This I understood too late. I have often told lies; and even now.

AMOS: What is your real name?

ARGIA: I believe that the Lord, in a short time from now, will not be asking names of me; He will be asking what my profit has been. The only one I have had I have had this night. And so, not utterly bereft, but with a little coin I go before Him. [*She raises her head slightly, and her voice also.*] Only a little, but my own; not given to me, nor inherited; but mine. This is the profit that makes owners and possessors of us. I am sinning still; since of what I have done tonight I am a little proud: it is the single thing that I can tell about myself . . . [*Dropping her voice a little.*] I have great need that soon I shall meet someone who will listen to me. [*She turns.*]

[MAUPA *comes in, followed by the* PORTER.]

ARGIA: Now is it?

AMOS: Yes.

[MAUPA *goes over to take the child from her.* ARGIA *prevents him, hugging the child close.*]

AMOS [*motioning* MAUPA *to stand back*]: The child will return to where he has lived hitherto, and where no one is informed of who he is. [*He takes the child from* ARGIA.] The sentence will be carried out at once. Immediately afterwards, it will be announced that the woman known as the Queen is dead and that therefore the Unitary Government has triumphed, the actions of our enemies being now deprived of their aim.

[ARGIA *moves towards the door, preceded by* MAUPA.]

ARGIA: I believe that God . . . has intentionally made us, not docile, for that He would find useless . . . but different from Himself and a little too proud . . . so that we may . . . stand against Him, thwart Him, amaze Him . . . Perhaps that is His purpose. [*She takes another step forward.*] It is a long struggle. Only at the end do we find reconciliation; and rest. [*She looks at the child.*] I go away rich. I have acquired a son . . . and memories . . . If even a little memory survives in us, this night, for me, shall shine indeed. [*She shows her hand to* AMOS.] Tell them to leave this ring on my finger. [*She holds out a hand to the child.*] Good-bye, my sweet.

[*The child also puts a hand towards her.* ARGIA *turns to go towards the door; pauses in momentary bewilderment; extracts her lipstick, and puts a little on her lips.*]

ARGIA: My mouth was rather pale. [*She is now at the door.*] How lovely and serene it is over the mountains; and the star Diana is still there in the sky. Unquestionably, this is a seat for kings, and in it we must try to live regally.

[*She goes out. There is a silence. Suddenly the* PORTER *runs out after her.* AMOS, *listening, puts his hands over the child's ears.*

A burst of gun-fire is heard. ARGIA *is dead.*]

CURTAIN

JEAN-PAUL SARTRE

In Camera

Huis clos

TRANSLATED BY
STUART GILBERT

IN CAMERA

Huis clos (under the title of *Vicious Circle* in a translation by
Marjorie Gabain and Joan Swinstead) was performed at the
Arts Theatre Club, London, on 16 July 1946, with the
following cast:

VALET	Donald Pleasance
GARCIN	Alec Guinness
ESTELLE	Betty Ann Davies
INEZ	Beatrix Lehmann

The play was produced by Peter Brook

A drawing-room in Second Empire style. A massive bronze group stands on the mantelpiece.

GARCIN [*enters, accompanied by the* ROOM-VALET, *and glances round him*]: Mm! So here we are?

VALET: Yes, Mr Garcin.

GARCIN: And this is what it looks like?

VALET: Yes.

GARCIN: Second Empire furniture, I observe . . . Well, well, I dare say one gets used to it in time.

VALET: Some do. Some don't.

GARCIN: Are all the other rooms like this one?

VALET: How could they be? We cater for all sorts: Chinamen and Indians, for instance. What use would they have for a Second Empire chair?

GARCIN: And what use do you suppose *I* have for one? Do you know who I was? . . . Oh, well, it's no great matter. And, to tell the truth, I'd quite a habit of living amongst furniture that I didn't relish, and in false positions. I'd even come to like it. A false position in a Louis-Philippe dining-room – you know the style? – well, that had its points, you know. Bogus in bogus, so to speak.

VALET: And you'll find that living in a Second Empire drawing-room has its points.

GARCIN: Really? . . . Yes, yes, I dare say . . . [*He takes another look round.*] Still, I certainly didn't expect – this! You know what they tell us down there?

VALET: What about?

GARCIN: About [*makes a sweeping gesture*] this – er – residence.

VALET: Really, sir, how could you believe such cock-and-bull stories? Told by people who'd never set foot here. For, of course, if they had . . .

GARCIN: Quite so. [*Both laugh. Abruptly the laugh dies from* GARCIN'S *face.*] But, I say, where are the instruments of torture?

VALET: The what?

GARCIN: The racks and red-hot pincers and all the other paraphernalia?

VALET: Ah, you must have your little joke, sir!

GARCIN: My little joke? Oh, I see. No. I wasn't joking. [*A short silence. He strolls round the room.*] No mirrors, I notice. No windows. Only to be expected. And nothing breakable. [*Bursts out angrily*]. But, damn it all, they might have left me my toothbrush!

VALET: That's good! So you haven't yet got over your – what-do-you-call-it? – sense of human dignity? Excuse me smiling.

GARCIN [*thumping ragefully the arm of an armchair*]: I'll ask you to be more polite. I quite realize the position I'm in, but I won't tolerate . . .

VALET: Sorry, sir. No offence meant. But all our guests ask me the same questions. Silly questions, if you'll pardon me saying so. Where's the torture-chamber? That's the first thing they ask, all of them. They don't bother their heads about the bathroom requisites, that I can assure you. But, after a bit, when they've got their nerve back, they start in about their toothbrushes and what-not. Good heavens, Mr Garcin, can't you use your brains? What, I ask you, would be the point of brushing your teeth?

GARCIN [*more calmly*]: Yes, of course you're right. [*He looks round again.*] And why should one want to see oneself in a looking-glass? But that bronze contraption on the mantelpiece, that's another story. I suppose there will be times when I stare my eyes out at it. Stare my eyes out – see what I mean? . . . All right, let's put our cards on the table. I assure you I'm quite conscious of my position. Shall I tell you what it feels like? A man's drowning, choking, sinking by inches, till only his eyes are just above water. And what does he see? A bronze atrocity by – what's the fellow's name? – Barbedienne. A collector's piece. Like in a nightmare. That's their idea, isn't it? . . . No, I suppose you're under orders not to answer questions; and I won't insist. But don't forget, my man, I've a shrewd notion of what's coming to me, so don't you boast you've caught me off my guard. I'm facing up to the situation, facing up. [*He starts pacing the room again.*] So that's that; no toothbrush. And no bed, either. One never sleeps, I take it?

VALET: That's so.

GARCIN: Just as I expected. *Why* should one sleep? A sort of drowsiness steals on you, tickles you behind the ears, and you feel your eyes closing – but why sleep? You lie down on the sofa and . . . in a flash, sleep flies away. Miles and miles away. So you rub your eyes, get up, and it starts all over again.

VALET: Romantic, that's what you are.

GARCIN: Will you keep quiet, please! . . . I won't make a scene, I shan't be sorry for myself, I'll face up to the situation, as I said just now. Face it fairly and squarely. I won't have it springing at me from behind, before I've time to size it up. And you call that being 'romantic'! . . . So it comes to this; one doesn't need rest. Why bother about sleep if one isn't sleepy? That stands to reason, doesn't it? Wait a bit, there's a snag somewhere; something disagreeable. Why, now, should it be disagreeable? . . . Ah, I see; it's life without a break.

VALET: What do you mean by that?

GARCIN: What do I mean? [*Eyes the* VALET *suspiciously.*] I thought as much. That's why there's something so beastly, so damn' bad-mannered, in the way you stare at me. They're paralysed.

VALET: What are you talking about?

GARCIN: Your eyelids. We move ours up and down. Blinking, we call it. It's like a small black shutter that clicks down, and makes a break. Everything goes black; one's eyes are moistened. You can't imagine how restful, refreshing, it is. Four thousand little rests per hour. Four thousand little respites – just think! . . . So that's the idea. I'm to live without eyelids. Don't act the fool, you know what I mean. No eyelids, no sleep; it follows, doesn't it? I shall never sleep again. But then – how shall I endure my own company? Try to understand. You see, I'm fond of teasing, it's a second nature with me – and I'm used to teasing myself. Plaguing myself, if you prefer; I don't tease nicely. But I can't go on doing that without a break. Down there I had my nights. I slept. I always had good nights. By way of compensation, I suppose. And happy little dreams. There was a green field. Just an ordinary field. I used to stroll in it . . . Is it daytime now?

VALET: Can't you see? The lights are on.

GARCIN: Ah yes, I've got it. It's *your* daytime. And outside?

VALET: Outside?

GARCIN: Damn it, you know what I mean. Beyond that wall.

VALET: There's a passage.

GARCIN: And at the end of the passage?

VALET: There's more rooms, more passages and stairs.

GARCIN: And what lies beyond them?

VALET: That's all.

GARCIN: But surely you have a day off sometimes. Where do you go?

VALET: To my uncle's place. He's the head valet here. He has a room on the third floor.

GARCIN: I should have guessed as much. Where's the light-switch?

VALET: There isn't any.

GARCIN: What? Can't one turn off the light?

VALET: Oh, the management can cut off the current, if they want to. But I can't remember their having done so on this floor. We have all the electricity we want.

GARCIN: So one has to live with one's eyes open all the time?

VALET: To *live*, did you say?

GARCIN: Don't let's quibble over words. With one's eyes open. For ever. Always broad daylight in my eyes ... and in my head. [*Short silence.*] And suppose I took that contraption on the mantelpiece and dropped it on the lamp – wouldn't it go out?

VALET: You can't move it. It's too heavy.

GARCIN [*seizing the bronze ornament and trying to lift it*]: You're right. It's too heavy.

[*A short silence follows.*]

VALET: Very well, sir, if you don't need me any more, I'll be off.

GARCIN: What? You're going? [*The* VALET *goes up to the door.*] Wait. [VALET *looks round.*] That's a bell, isn't it? [VALET *nods.*] And if I ring, you're bound to come?

VALET: Well, yes, that's so – in a way. But you can never be sure about that bell. There's something wrong with the wiring, and it doesn't always work.

[GARCIN *goes to the bell-push and presses the button. A bell purrs outside.*]

GARCIN: It's working all right.

VALET [*looking surprised*]: So it is. [*He, too, presses the button.*] But I shouldn't count on it too much if I were you. It's ... capricious. Well, I really must go now. [GARCIN *makes a gesture to detain him.*] Yes, sir?

GARCIN: No, never mind. [*He goes to the mantelpiece and picks up a paper-knife.*] What's this?

VALET: Can't you see? An ordinary paper-knife.

GARCIN: Are there books here?

VALET: No.

GARCIN: Then what's the use of this? [VALET *shrugs his shoulders.*] Very well. You can go. [VALET *goes out.*]

[GARCIN *is by himself. He goes to the bronze ornament and strokes it reflectively. He sits down: then gets up, goes to the bell-push and presses the button. The bell remains silent. He tries two or three times, without success. Then he tries to open the door, also without success. He calls the* VALET *several times, but gets no result. He beats the door with his fists, still calling. Suddenly he grows calm and sits down again. At the same moment the door opens and* INEZ *enters, followed by the* VALET.]

VALET: Did you call, sir?

GARCIN [*on the point of answering* 'Yes' – *but then his eyes fall on* INEZ.]: No.

VALET [*turning to* INEZ]: This is your room, madam. [INEZ *says nothing.*] If there's any information you require . . .? [INEZ *still keeps silent, and the* VALET *looks slightly huffed.*] Most of our guests have quite a lot to ask me. But I won't insist. Anyhow, as regards the toothbrush, and the electric bell, and that thing on the mantelshelf, this gentleman can tell you anything you want to know, as well as I could. We've had a little chat, him and me. [VALET *goes out.*] [GARCIN *refrains from looking at* INEZ, *who is inspecting the room. Abruptly she turns to* GARCIN.]

INEZ: Where's Florence? [GARCIN *does not reply.*] Didn't you hear? I asked you about Florence. Where is she?

GARCIN: I haven't an idea.

INEZ: Ah, that's the way it works, is it? Torture by separation. Well, as far as I'm concerned, you won't get anywhere. Florence was a tiresome little fool, and I shan't miss her in the least.

GARCIN: I beg your pardon. Who do you suppose I am?

INEZ: You? Why, the torturer, of course.

GARCIN [*looks startled, then bursts out laughing*]: Well, that's a good one! Too comic for words, I, the torturer! So you came in, had a look at me, and thought I was – er – one of the staff. Of course it's that silly fellow's fault; he should have introduced us. A torturer indeed! I'm Joseph Garcin, journalist and man of letters by profession.

And as we're both in the same boat, so to speak, might I ask you, Mrs . . .?

INEZ [*testily*]: Not 'Mrs'. I'm unmarried.

GARCIN: Right. That's a start anyway. Well, now that we've broken the ice, do you *really* think I look like a torturer . . .? And, by the way, how does one recognize torturers when one sees them? Evidently you've ideas on the subject.

INEZ: They look frightened.

GARCIN: Frightened! But how ridiculous! Of whom should they be frightened? Of their victims?

INEZ: Laugh away, but I know what I'm talking about. I've often watched my face in the glass.

GARCIN: In the glass? [*He looks round him.*] How beastly of them! They've removed everything in the least resembling a glass. [*Short silence.*] Anyhow, I can assure you I'm not frightened. Not that I take my position lightly; I realize its gravity only too well. But I'm not afraid.

INEZ [*shrugging her shoulders*]: That's your affair. [*Silence.*] Must you be here all the time, or do you take a stroll outside now and then?

GARCIN: The door's locked.

INEZ: Oh! . . . That's too bad.

GARCIN: I can quite understand that it bores you having me here. And I, too – well, quite frankly, I'd rather be alone. I want to think things out, you know; to set my life in order, and one does that better by oneself. But I'm sure we'll manage to pull along together somehow. I'm no talker, I don't move much; in fact I'm a peaceful sort of fellow. Only, if I may venture on a suggestion, we should make a point of being extremely courteous to each other. That will ease the situation for us both.

INEZ: I'm not polite.

GARCIN: Then I must be polite for two.

[*A longish silence.* GARCIN *is sitting on a sofa, while* INEZ *paces up and down the room.*]

INEZ [*fixing her eyes on him*]: Your mouth!

GARCIN [*as if waking from a dream*]: I beg your pardon.

INEZ: Can't you keep your mouth still? You keep twisting it about all the time. It's grotesque.

GARCIN: So sorry. I wasn't aware of it.

INEZ: That's just what I reproach you with. [GARCIN'S *mouth twitches.*] There you are! You talk about politeness, and you don't even try to control your face. Remember you're not alone; you've no right to inflict the sight of your fear on me.

GARCIN [*getting up and going towards her*]: How about you? Aren't you afraid?

INEZ: What would be the use? There was some point in being afraid *before*; while one still had hope.

GARCIN [*in a low voice*]: There's no more hope – but it's still 'before'. We haven't yet begun to suffer.

INEZ: That's so. [*A short silence.*] Well? What's going to happen?

GARCIN: I don't know. I'm waiting.

[*Silence again.* GARCIN *sits down and* INEZ *resumes her pacing up and down the room.* GARCIN'S *mouth twitches; after a glance at* INEZ *he buries his face in his hands. Enter* ESTELLE *with the* VALET. ESTELLE *looks at* GARCIN, *whose face is still hidden by his hands.*]

ESTELLE [*to* GARCIN]: No! Don't look up. I know what you're hiding with your hands. I know you've no face left. [GARCIN *removes his hands.*] What! [*A short pause. Then, in a tone of surprise.*] But I don't know you!

GARCIN: I'm not the torturer, madam.

ESTELLE: I never thought you were. I . . . I thought someone was trying to play a rather nasty trick on me. [*To the* VALET.] Is anyone else coming?

VALET: No, madam. No one else is coming.

ESTELLE: Oh! Then we're to stay by ourselves, the three of us, this gentleman, this lady, and myself. [*She starts laughing.*]

GARCIN [*angrily*]: There's nothing to laugh about.

ESTELLE [*still laughing*]: It's those sofas. They're so hideous. And just look how they've been arranged. It makes me think of New Year's Day – when I used to visit that boring old aunt of mine, Aunt Mary. Her house is full of horrors like that . . . I suppose each of us has a sofa of his own. Is that one mine? [*To the* VALET.] But you can't expect me to sit on that one. It would be too horrible for words. I'm in pale blue and it's vivid green.

INEZ: Would you prefer mine?

ESTELLE: That claret-coloured one, you mean? That's very sweet of you, but really – no, I don't think it'd be so much better. What's the good of worrying, anyhow? We've got to take what comes to us, and I'll stick to the green one. [*Pauses.*] The only one which might do, at a pinch, is that gentleman's. [*Another pause.*]

INEZ: Did you hear, Mr Garcin?

GARCIN [*with a slight start*]: Oh . . . the sofa, you mean. So sorry. [*He rises.*] Please take it, madam.

ESTELLE: Thanks. [*She takes off her coat and drops it on the sofa. A short silence.*] Well, as we're to live together, I suppose we'd better introduce ourselves. My name's Rigault. Estelle Rigault. [GARCIN *bows and is going to announce his name, but* INEZ *steps in front of him.*]

INEZ: And I'm Inez Serrano. Very pleased to meet you.

GARCIN [*bowing again*]: Joseph Garcin.

VALET: Do you require me any longer?

ESTELLE: No, you can go. I'll ring when I want you.

[*Exit* VALET, *with polite bows to everyone.*]

INEZ: You're very pretty. I wish we'd had some flowers to welcome you with.

ESTELLE: Flowers? Yes, I loved flowers. Only they'd fade so quickly here, wouldn't they? It's so stuffy. Oh, well, the great thing is to keep as cheerful as we can, don't you agree? Of course, you, too, are . . .

INEZ: Yes. Last week. What about you?

ESTELLE: I'm . . . quite recent. Yesterday. As a matter of fact, the ceremony's not quite over. [*Her tone is natural enough, but she seems to be seeing what she describes.*] The wind's blowing my sister's veil all over the place. She's trying her best to cry. Come, dear! Make another effort. That's better. Two tears, two teeny little tears are twinkling under the black veil. On dear! What a sight Olga looks this morning! She's holding my sister's arm, helping her along. She's not crying, and I don't blame her; tears always mess one's face up, don't they? Olga was my bosom friend, you know.

INEZ: Did you suffer much?

ESTELLE: No. I was only half-conscious, mostly.

INEZ: What was it?

ESTELLE: Pneumonia [*In the same tone as before.*] It's over now, they're leaving the cemetery. Good-bye. Good-bye. Quite a crowd they are. My husband's stayed at home. Prostrated with grief, poor man. [*To* INEZ.] How about you?

INEZ: The gas-stove.

ESTELLE: And you, Mr Garcin?

GARCIN: Twelve bullets through my chest. [ESTELLE *makes a horrified gesture.*] Sorry! I fear I'm not good company amongst the dead.

ESTELLE: Please, please don't use that word. It's so . . . so crude. In terribly bad taste, really. It doesn't mean much, anyhow. Somehow I feel we've never been so much alive as now. If we've absolutely got to mention this . . . this state of things, I suggest we call ourselves – wait! – absentees. Have you been . . . been absent for long?

GARCIN: About a month.

ESTELLE: Where do you come from?

GARCIN: From Rio.

ESTELLE: I'm from Paris. Have you anyone left down there?

GARCIN: Yes, my wife. [*In the same tone as* ESTELLE *has been using.*] She's waiting at the entrance of the barracks. She comes there every day. But they won't let her in. Now she's trying to peep between the bars. She doesn't yet know I'm . . . absent, but she suspects it. Now she's going away. She's wearing her black dress. So much the better, she won't need to change. She isn't crying, but she never did cry, anyhow. It's a bright sunny day and she's like a black shadow creeping down the empty street. Those big tragic eyes of hers – with that martyred look they always had. Oh, how she got on my nerves!

[*A short silence.* GARCIN *sits on the central sofa, and buries his head in his hands.*]

INEZ: Estelle!

ESTELLE: Please, Mr Garcin!

GARCIN: What is it?

ESTELLE: You're sitting on my sofa.

GARCIN: I beg your pardon. [*He gets up.*]

ESTELLE: You looked so . . . so far away. Sorry I disturbed you.

GARCIN: I was setting my life in order. [INEZ *starts laughing.*] You may laugh, but you'd do better to follow my example.

INEZ: No need. My life's in perfect order. It tidied itself up nicely of its own accord. So I needn't bother about it now.

GARCIN: Really? You imagine it's so simple as that. [*He runs his hand over his forehead.*] Whew! How hot it is here! Do you mind if . . .? [*He begins taking off his coat.*]

ESTELLE: How dare you! [*More gently.*] No, please don't. I loathe men in their shirt-sleeves.

GARCIN [*putting on his coat again*]: All right. [*A short pause.*] Of course I used to spend my nights in the newspaper office, and it was a regular Black Hole, so we never kept our coats on. Stiflingly hot it could be. [*Short pause. In the same tone as previously.*] Stifling, that it *is*. It's night now.

ESTELLE: That's so. Olga's undressing; it must be after midnight. How quickly the time passes, on earth!

INEZ: Yes, after midnight. They've sealed up my room. It's dark, pitch dark, and empty.

GARCIN: They've slung their coats on the backs of the chairs and rolled up their shirt-sleeves above the elbow. The air stinks of men and cigar-smoke. [*A short silence.*] I used to like living amongst men in their shirt-sleeves.

ESTELLE [*aggressively*]: Well, in that case our tastes differ. That's all it proves. [*Turning to* INEZ.] What about you? Do you like men in their shirt-sleeves?

INEZ: Oh, I don't care much for men, anyway.

ESTELLE [*looking at the other two with a puzzled air*]: Really I can't imagine why they put us three together. It doesn't make sense.

INEZ [*stifling a laugh*]: What's that you said?

ESTELLE: I'm looking at you two and thinking that we're going to live together . . . It's so absurd. I expected to meet old friends, or relatives.

INEZ: Yes, a charming old friend – with a hole in the middle of his face.

ESTELLE: Yes, him too. He danced the tango so divinely. Like a professional . . . But why, why should we of all people be put together?

GARCIN: A pure fluke, I should say. They lodge folks as they can, in the order of their coming. [*To* INEZ.] Why are you laughing?

INEZ: Because you amuse me, with your 'flukes'. As if they left anything to chance! But I suppose you've got to reassure yourself somehow.

ESTELLE [*hesitantly*]: I wonder now. Don't you think we may have met each other at some time in our lives?

INEZ: Never. I shouldn't have forgotten you.

ESTELLE: Or perhaps we have friends in common. I wonder if you know the Dubois-Seymours?

INEZ: Not likely.

ESTELLE: But *everyone* went to their parties.

INEZ: What's their job?

ESTELLE: Oh, they don't do anything. But they have a lovely house in the country, and hosts of people visit them.

INEZ: I didn't. I was a post-office clerk.

ESTELLE [*recoiling a little*]: Ah, yes ... Of course, in that case ... [*A pause.*] And you, Mr Garcin?

GARCIN: We've never met. I always lived in Rio.

ESTELLE: Then you must be right. It's mere chance that has brought us together.

INEZ: Mere chance? Then it's by chance this room is furnished as we see it. It's an accident that the sofa on the right is a livid green, and that one on the left's wine-red. Mere chance? Well, just try to shift the sofas and you'll see the difference quick enough. And that thing on the mantelpiece, do you think it's there by accident? And what about the heat here? How about that? [*A short silence.*] I tell you they've thought it all out. Down to the last detail. Nothing was left to chance. This room was all set for us.

ESTELLE: But really! Everything here's so hideous; all in angles, so uncomfortable. I always loathed angles.

INEZ [*shrugging his shoulders*]: And do you think *I* lived in a Second Empire drawing-room?

ESTELLE: So it was all fixed up beforehand?

INEZ: Yes. And they've put us together deliberately.

ESTELLE: Then it's not mere chance that *you* precisely are sitting opposite *me*? But what can be the idea behind it?

INEZ: Ask me another! I only know they're waiting.

ESTELLE: I never could bear the idea of anyone's expecting something from me. It always made me want to do just the opposite.

INEZ: Well, do it, if you can. You don't even know what they expect.

ESTELLE [*stamping her foot*]: It's outrageous! So something's coming to me from you two? [*She eyes each in turn.*] Something nasty, I suppose. There are some faces that tell me everything at once. Yours don't convey anything.

GARCIN [*turning abruptly towards* INEZ]: Look here! Why are we together? You've given us quite enough hints, you may as well come out with it.

INEZ [*in a surprised tone*]: But I know nothing, absolutely nothing about it. I'm as much in the dark as you are.

GARCIN: We've *got* to know. [*Ponders for a while.*]

INEZ: If only each of us had the guts to tell . . .

GARCIN: Tell what?

INEZ: Estelle!

ESTELLE: Yes?

INEZ: What have you done? I mean, why have they sent you here?

ESTELLE [*quickly*]: That's just it. I haven't a notion, not the foggiest. In fact I'm wondering if there hasn't been some ghastly mistake. [*To* INEZ.] Don't smile. Just think of the number of people who . . . who become absentees every day. There must be thousands and thousands, and probably they're sorted out by – by understrappers, you know what I mean. Stupid employees who don't know their job. So they're bound to make mistakes sometimes . . . Do stop smiling. [*To* GARCIN.] Why don't you speak? If they made a mistake in my case, they may have done the same about you. [*To* INEZ.] And you, too. Anyhow, isn't it better to think we've got here by mistake?

INEZ: Is that all you have to tell us?

ESTELLE: What else should I tell? I've nothing to hide. I lost my parents when I was a kid, and I had my young brother to bring up. We were terribly poor and when an old friend of my people asked me to marry him I said 'Yes'. He was very well off, and quite nice. My brother was a very delicate child and needed all sorts of attention, so really that was the right thing for me to do, don't you agree? My husband was old enough to be my father, but for six years we had a happy married life. Then two years ago I met the man I was fated to love. We knew in the moment we set eyes on each other. He asked me to run away with him, and I refused. Then I got pneumonia and it finished me. That's the whole story. No doubt, by certain standards, I did wrong to sacrifice my youth to a man nearly three times my age. [*To* GARCIN.] Do *you* think that could be called a sin?

GARCIN: Certainly not. [*A short silence.*] And now, tell me, do you think it's a crime to stand by one's principles?

ESTELLE: Of course not. Surely no one could blame a man for that!

GARCIN: Wait a bit! I ran a pacifist newspaper. Then war broke out. What was I to do? Everyone was watching me, wondering, 'Will he dare?' Well, I dared. I folded my arms and they shot me. Had I done anything wrong?

ESTELLE [*laying her hand on his arm*]: Wrong? On the contrary. You were . . .

INEZ [*breaks in ironically*]: . . . a hero! And how about your wife, Mr Garcin?

GARCIN: That's simple. I'd rescued her from . . . from the gutter.

ESTELLE [*to* INEZ]: You see! You see!

INEZ: Yes, I see. [*A pause.*] Look here! What's the point of play-acting, trying to throw dust in each other's eyes? We're all tarred with the same brush.

ESTELLE [*indignantly*]: How dare you!

INEZ: Yes, we are criminals – murderers – all three of us. We're in hell, my pets, they never make mistakes, and people aren't damned for nothing.

ESTELLE: Stop! For heaven's sake . . .

INEZ: In hell! Damned souls – that's us, all three!

ESTELLE: Keep quiet! I forbid you to use such disgusting words.

INEZ: A damned soul – that's you, my little plaster saint. And ditto our friend there, the noble pacifist. We've had our hour of pleasure, haven't we? There have been people who burnt their lives out for our sakes – and we chuckled over it. So now we have to pay the reckoning.

GARCIN [*raising his fist*]: Will you keep your mouth shut, damn it!

INEZ [*confronting him fearlessly, but with a look of vast surprise*]: Well, well! [*A pause.*] Ah, I understand now. I know why they've put us three together.

GARCIN: I advise you to . . . to think twice before you say any more.

INEZ: Wait! You'll see how simple it is. Childishly simple. Obviously there aren't any physical torments – you agree, don't you? And yet we're in hell. And no one else will come here. We'll stay in this room together, the three of us, for ever and ever . . . In short, there's someone absent here, the official torturer.

GARCIN [*sotto voce*]: I'd noticed that.

INEZ: It's obvious what they're after – an economy of man-power . . . or devil-power, if you prefer. The same idea as in the cafeteria where customers serve themselves.

ESTELLE: What ever do you mean?

INEZ: I mean that each of us will act as torturer of the two others.

[*There is a short silence, while they digest this information.*]

GARCIN [*gently*]: No, I shall never be your torturer. I wish neither of you any harm, and I've no concern with you. None at all. So the solution's easy enough; each of us stays put in his or her corner, and takes no notice of the others. You here, you here, and I there. Like soldiers at our posts. Also, we mustn't speak. Not one word. That won't be difficult; each of us has plenty of material for self-communings. I think I could stay ten thousand years with only my thoughts for company.

ESTELLE: Have *I* got to keep silent, too?

GARCIN: Yes. And that way we . . . we'll work out our salvation. Looking into ourselves, never raising our heads. Agreed?

INEZ: Agreed.

ESTELLE [*after some hesitation*]: I agree.

GARCIN: Then . . . Good-bye.

[*He goes to his sofa, and buries his head in his hands. There is a long silence; then* INEZ *begins singing to herself.*]

INEZ: [*Singing.*]

> What a crowd in Whitefriars Lane!
> They've set trestles in a row,
> With a scaffold and the knife,
> And a pail of bran below.
> Come, good folks, to Whitefriars Lane,
> Come to see the merry show!
>
> The headsman rose at crack of dawn,
> He'd a long day's work in hand,
> Chopping heads off generals,
> Priests and peers and admirals,
> All the highest in the land.
> What a crowd in Whitefriars Lane!

See them standing in a line,
Ladies all dressed up so fine.
But their heads have got to go,
Heads and hats roll down below.
Come, good folks, to Whitefriars Lane
Come to see the merry show!

[*Meanwhile* ESTELLE *has been plying her powder-puff and lipstick. She looks round for a mirror, fumbles in her bag, then turns towards* GARCIN.]

ESTELLE: Excuse me, have you a glass? [GARCIN *does not answer.*] Any sort of glass, a pocket-mirror will do. [GARCIN *remains silent.*] Even if you won't speak to me, you might lend me a glass.

[*His head still buried in his hands,* GARCIN *ignores her.*]

INEZ [*eagerly*]: Don't worry! I've a glass in my bag. [*She opens her bag. Angrily.*] It's gone! They must have taken it from me at the entrance.

ESTELLE: How tiresome!

[*A short silence.* ESTELLE *shuts her eyes and sways, as if about to faint.* INEZ *runs forward and holds her up.*]

INEZ: What's the matter?

ESTELLE [*opens her eyes and smiles*]: I feel so queer. [*She pats herself.*] Don't you ever get taken that way? When I can't see myself I begin to wonder if I really and truly exist. I pat myself just to make sure, but it doesn't help much.

INEZ: You're lucky. I'm always conscious of myself – in my mind. Painfully conscious.

ESTELLE: Ah yes, in your mind. But everything that goes on in one's head is so vague, isn't it? It makes one want to sleep. [*She is silent for a while.*] I've six big mirrors in my bedroom. There they are. I can see them. But they don't see me. They're reflecting the carpet, the settee, the window . . . but how empty it is, a glass in which I'm absent. When I talked to people I always made sure there was one near by in which I could see myself. I watched myself talking. And somehow it kept me alert, seeing myself as the others saw me . . . Oh dear! My lipstick! I'm sure I've put it on all crooked. No, I can't do without a looking-glass for ever and ever, I simply can't.

INEZ: Suppose I try to be your glass? Come and pay me a visit, dear. Here's a place for you on my sofa.

ESTELLE: But – [*Points to* GARCIN.]

INEZ: Oh, he doesn't count.

ESTELLE: But we're going to . . . to hurt each other. You said it yourself.

INEZ: Do I look as if I wanted to hurt you?

ESTELLE: One never can tell.

INEZ: Much more likely *you'll* hurt *me*. Still, what does it matter? If I've got to suffer, it may as well be at your hands, your pretty hands. Sit down. Come closer. Closer. Look into my eyes. What do you see?

ESTELLE: Oh, I'm there! But so tiny I can't see myself properly.

INEZ: But *I* can. Every inch of you. Now ask me questions. I'll be as candid as any looking-glass.

[ESTELLE *seems rather embarrassed and turns to* GARCIN, *as if appealing to him for help.*]

ESTELLE: Please, Mr Garcin. Sure our chatter isn't boring you?

[GARCIN *makes no reply.*]

INEZ: Don't worry about him. As I said, he doesn't count. We're by ourselves . . . Ask away.

ESTELLE: Are my lips all right?

INEZ: Show! No, they're a bit smudgy.

ESTELLE: I thought as much. Luckily [*throws a quick glance at* GARCIN] no one's seen me. I'll try again.

INEZ: That's better. No. Follow the line of your lips. Wait! I'll guide your hand. There. That's quite good.

ESTELLE: As good as when I came in?

INEZ: Far better. Crueller. Your mouth looks quite diabolical that way.

ESTELLE: Good gracious! And you say you like it! How maddening, not being able to see for myself! You're quite sure, Miss Serrano, that it's all right now?

INEZ: Won't you call me Inez?

ESTELLE: Are you sure it looks all right?

INEZ: You're lovely, Estelle.

ESTELLE: But how can I rely upon your taste? Is it the same as *my* taste? Oh, how sickening it all is, enough to drive one crazy!

INEZ: I *have* your taste, my dear, because I like you so much. Look at me. No, straight. Now smile. I'm not so ugly, either. Aren't I nicer than your glass?

ESTELLE: Oh, I don't know. You scare me rather. My reflection in the glass never did that; of course I knew it so well. Like something I had tamed . . . I'm going to smile, and my smile will sink down into your pupils, and heaven knows what it will become.

INEZ: And why shouldn't you 'tame' *me*? [*The women gaze at each other*, ESTELLE *with a sort of fearful fascination.*] Listen! I want you to call me 'Inez'. We must be great friends.

ESTELLE: I don't make friends with women very easily.

INEZ: Not with postal clerks, you mean? Hullo, what's that – that nasty red spot at the bottom of your cheek? A pimple?

ESTELLE: A pimple? Oh, how simply foul! Where?

INEZ: There . . . You know the way they catch larks – with a mirror? I'm your lark-mirror, my dear, and you can't escape me . . . There isn't any pimple, not a trace of one. So what about it? Suppose the mirror started telling lies? Or suppose I covered my eyes – as he is doing – and refused to look at you, all that loveliness of yours would be wasted on the desert air. No, don't be afraid, I can't help looking at you, I shan't turn my eyes away. And I'll be nice to you, ever so nice. Only you must be nice to me, too.

[*A short silence.*]

ESTELLE: Are you really . . . attracted by me?

INEZ: Very much indeed.

[*Another short silence.*]

ESTELLE [*indicating* GARCIN *by a slight movement of her head*]: But I wish he'd notice me, too.

INEZ: Of course! Because he's a Man! [*To* GARCIN.] You've won. [GARCIN *says nothing.*] But look at her, damn it! [*Still no reply from* GARCIN.] Don't pretend. You haven't missed a word of what we've said.

GARCIN: Quite so; not a word. I stuck my fingers in my ears, but your voices thudded in my brain. Silly chatter. Now will you leave me in peace, you two? I'm not interested in you.

INEZ: Not in me, perhaps – but how about this child? Aren't you interested in her? Oh, I saw through your game; you got on your high horse just to impress her.

GARCIN: I asked you to leave me in peace. There's someone talking about me in the newspaper office and I want to listen. And, if it'll make you any happier, let me tell you that I've no use for the 'child', as you call her.

ESTELLE: Thanks.

GARCIN: Oh, I didn't mean it rudely.

ESTELLE: You cad!

[*They confront each other in silence for some moments.*]

GARCIN: So that's that. [*Pause.*] You know I begged you not to speak.

ESTELLE: It's *her* fault; she started. I didn't ask anything of her and she came and offered me her . . . her glass.

INEZ: So you say. But all the time you were making up to him, trying every trick to catch his attention.

ESTELLE: Well, why shouldn't I?

GARCIN: You're crazy, both of you. Don't you see where this is leading us? For pity's sake, keep your mouths shut. [*Pause.*] Now let's all sit down again quite quietly; we'll look at the floor and each must try to forget the others are there.

[*A longish silence.* GARCIN *sits down. The women return hesitantly to their places. Suddenly* INEZ *swings round on him.*]

INEZ: To forget about the others? How utterly absurd! I *feel* you there, down to my marrow. Your silence clamours in my ears. You can nail up your mouth, cut your tongue out – but you can't prevent your *being there*. Can you stop your thoughts? I hear them ticking away like a clock, tick-tock, tick-tock, and I'm certain you hear mine. It's all very well skulking on your sofa, but you're everywhere, and every sound comes to me soiled, because you've intercepted it on its way. Why, you've even stolen my face; you know it and I don't! And what about her, about Estelle? You've stolen her from me, too; if she and I were alone, do you suppose she'd treat me as she does? No, take your hands from your face, I won't leave you in peace – that would suit your book too well. You'd go on sitting there, in a sort of trance, like a Yogi, and even if I didn't see her I'd feel it in my bones – that she was making every sound, even the rustle of her dress, for your benefit, throwing you smiles you didn't see . . . Well, I won't stand for that, I prefer to choose my hell; I prefer to look you in the eyes, and fight it out face to face.

GARCIN: Have it your own way. I suppose we were bound to come to this; they knew what they were about, and we're easy game. If they'd put me in a room with men . . . men can keep their mouths shut. But it's no use wanting the impossible. [*He goes to* ESTELLE *and lightly fondles her neck.*] So I attract you, little girl? It seems you were making eyes at me?

ESTELLE: Don't touch me.

GARCIN: Why not? We might, anyhow, be natural . . . Do you know, I used to be mad keen on women? And some were fond of me. So we may as well stop posing, we've nothing to lose. Why trouble about politeness, and decorum, and the rest of it? We're between ourselves. And presently we shall be naked as – as newborn babes.

ESTELLE: Oh, let me be!

GARCIN: As new-born babes. Well, I'd warned you, anyhow. I asked so little of you, nothing but peace and a little silence. I'd put my fingers in my ears. Gomez was spouting away as usual, standing in the centre of the room, with all the pressmen listening. In their shirtsleeves. I tried to hear, but it wasn't too easy. Things on earth move so quickly, you know. Couldn't you have held your tongues? Now it's over, he's stopped talking, and what he thinks of me has gone back into his head. Well, we've got to see it through somehow . . . Naked as we were born. So much the better; I want to know whom I have to deal with.

INEZ: You know already. There's nothing more to learn.

GARCIN: You're wrong. So long as each of us hasn't made a clean breast of it – why they've damned him or her – we know nothing. Nothing that counts. You, young lady, you shall begin. Why? Tell us why. If you are frank, if we bring our spectres into the open, it may save us from disaster. So – out with it! Why?

ESTELLE: I tell you I haven't a notion. They wouldn't tell me why.

GARCIN: That's so. They wouldn't tell me, either. But I've a pretty shrewd idea . . . Perhaps you're shy of speaking first? Right. I'll lead off. [*A short silence.*] I'm not a very estimable person.

INEZ: No need to tell us that. We know you were a deserter.

GARCIN: Let that be. It's only a side-issue. I'm here because I treated my wife abominably. That's all. For five years. Naturally, she's suffering still. There she is: the moment I mention her, I see her. It's Gomez who interests me, and it's she I see. Where's Gomez got to? For five years. There! They've given her back my things; she's sitting by the window, with my coat on her knees. The coat with the twelve bullet-holes. The blood's like rust; a brown ring round each hole. It's quite a museum-piece, that coat; scarred with history. And I used to wear it, fancy! . . . Now, can't you shed a tear, my love? Surely you'll squeeze one out – at last? No? You can't manage it? . . . Night after night I came home blind drunk; stinking of wine and women. She'd sat up for me, of course. But she never cried, never uttered a word of reproach. Only her eyes spoke. Big, tragic eyes. I don't regret anything. I must pay the price, but I shan't whine . . . It's snowing in the street. Won't you cry, confound you! That woman was a born martyr, you know; a victim by vocation.

INEZ [*almost tenderly*]: Why did you hurt her like that?

GARCIN: It was so easy. A word was enough to make her flinch. Like a sensitive plant. But never, never a reproach. I'm fond of teasing. I watched and waited. But no, not a tear, not a protest. I'd picked her up out of the gutter, you understand . . . Now she's stroking the coat. Her eyes are shut and she's feeling with her fingers for the bullet-holes. What are you after? What do you expect? I tell you I regret nothing. The truth is, she admired me too much. Does that mean anything to you?

INEZ: No. Nobody admired *me*.

GARCIN: So much the better. So much the better for you. I suppose all this strikes you as very vague. Well, here's something you can get your teeth into. I brought a half-caste girl to stay in our house. My wife slept upstairs; she must have heard . . . everything. She was an early riser and, as I and the girl stayed in bed late, she served us our morning coffee.

INEZ: You brute!

GARCIN: Yes, a brute, if you like. But a well-beloved brute. [*A far-away look comes to his eyes.*] No, it's nothing. Only Gomez, and he's not talking about *me* . . . What were you saying? Yes, a brute. Certainly. Else why should I be here? [*To* INEZ.] Your turn.

INEZ: Well, I was what some people down there called 'a damned bitch'. Damned already. So it's no surprise, being here.

GARCIN: Is that all you have to say?

INEZ: No. There was that affair with Florence. A dead men's tale. With three corpses to it. He to start with; then she and I. So there's no one left, I've nothing to worry about; it was a clean sweep. Only that room. I see it now and then. Empty, with the doors locked . . .

No, they've just unlocked them. 'To let.' It's to let; there's a notice on the door. That's . . . too ridiculous.

GARCIN: Three: Three deaths, you said?

INEZ: Three.

GARCIN: One man and two women?

INEZ: Yes.

GARCIN: Well, well. [*A pause.*] Did he kill himself?

INEZ: He? No, he hadn't the guts for that. Still, he'd every reason; we led him a dog's life. As a matter of fact he was run over by a tram. A silly sort of end . . . I was living with them; he was my cousin.

GARCIN: Was Florence fair?

INEZ: Fair? [*Glances at* ESTELLE.] You know, I don't regret a thing; still, I'm not so very keen on telling you the story.

GARCIN: That's all right . . . So you got sick of him?

INEZ: Quite gradually. All sorts of little things got on my nerves. For instance, he made a noise when he was drinking – a sort of gurgle. Trifles like that. He was rather pathetic really. Vulnerable. Why are you smiling?

GARCIN: Because I, anyhow, am *not* vulnerable.

INEZ: Don't be too sure . . . I crept inside her skin, she saw the world through my eyes. When she left him, I had her on my hands. We shared a bed-sitting-room at the other end of the town.

GARCIN: And then?

INEZ: Then that tram did its job. I used to remind her every day: 'Yes, my pet, we killed him between us.' [*A pause.*] I'm rather cruel, really.

GARCIN: So am I.

INEZ: No, you're not cruel. It's something else.

GARCIN: What?

INEZ: I'll tell you later. When I say I'm cruel, I mean I can't get on without making people suffer. Like a live coal. A live coal in others' hearts. When I'm alone I flicker out. For six months I flamed away in her heart, till there was nothing but a cinder. One night she got up and turned on the gas while I was asleep. Then she crept back into bed. So now you know.

GARCIN: Well! Well!

INEZ: Yes? What's in your mind.

GARCIN: Nothing. Only that it's not a pretty story.

INEZ: Obviously. But what matter?

GARCIN: As you say, what matter? [*To* ESTELLE.] Your turn. What have you done?

ESTELLE: As I told you, I haven't a notion. I rack my brain, but it's no use.

GARCIN: Right. Then we'll give you a hand. That fellow with the smashed face, who was he?

ESTELLE: Who . . . who do you mean?

INEZ: You know quite well. The man you were so scared of seeing when you came in.

ESTELLE: Oh, him! A friend of mine.

GARCIN: Why were you afraid of him?

ESTELLE: That's my business, Mr Garcin.

INEZ: Did he shoot himself on your account?

ESTELLE: Of course not. How absurd you are!

GARCIN: Then why should you have been so scared? He blew his brains out, didn't he? That's how his face got smashed.

ESTELLE: Don't! Please don't go on.

GARCIN: Because of you. Because of you.

INEZ: He shot himself because of you.

ESTELLE: Leave me alone! It's . . . it's not fair, bullying me like that. I want to go! I want to go!

[*She runs to the door and shakes it.*]

GARCIN: Go, if you can. Personally, I ask for nothing better. Unfortunately the door's locked.

[ESTELLE *presses the bell-push, but the bell does not ring.* INEZ *and* GARCIN *laugh.* ESTELLE *swings round on them, her back to the door.*]

ESTELLE [*in a muffled voice*]: You're hateful, both of you.

INEZ: Hateful? Yes, that's the word. Now, get on with it. That fellow who killed himself on your account – you were his mistress, eh?

GARCIN: Of course she was. And he wanted to have her to himself alone. That's so, isn't it?

INEZ: He danced the tango like a professional, but he was poor as a church mouse – that's right, isn't it?

[*A short silence.*]

GARCIN: Was he poor or not? Give a straight answer.

ESTELLE: Yes, he was poor.

GARCIN: And then you had your reputation to keep up. One day he came and implored you to run away with him, and you laughed in his face.

INEZ: That's it. You laughed at him. And so he killed himself.

ESTELLE: Used you to look at Florence in that way?

INEZ: Yes.

[*A short pause, then* ESTELLE *bursts out laughing.*]

ESTELLE: You've got it all wrong, you two. [*She stiffens her shoulders, still leaning against the door, and faces them. Her voice grows shrill, truculent.*] He wanted me to have a baby. So there!

GARCIN: And you didn't want one?

ESTELLE: I certainly didn't. But the baby came, worse luck. I went to Switzerland for five months. No one knew anything. It was a girl. Roger was with me when she was born. It pleased him no end, having a daughter. It didn't please *me*!

GARCIN: And then?

ESTELLE: There was a balcony overlooking the lake. I brought a big stone. He could see what I was up to, and he kept on shouting, 'Estelle, for God's sake, don't!' I hated him then. He saw it all. He was leaning over the balcony and he saw the rings spreading on the water . . .

GARCIN: Yes? And then?

ESTELLE: That's all. I came back to Paris – and he did as he wished.

GARCIN: You mean, he blew his brains out?

ESTELLE: It was absurd of him, really; my husband never suspected anything. [*A pause.*] Oh, how I loathe you! [*She sobs tearlessly.*]

GARCIN: Nothing doing. Tears don't flow in this place.

ESTELLE: I'm a coward. A coward! [*Pause.*] If you knew how I hate you!

INEZ [*taking her in her arms*]: Poor child! [*To* GARCIN.] So the hearing's over. But there's no need to look like a hanging judge.

GARCIN: A hanging judge? [*He glances round him.*] I'd give a lot to be able to see myself in a glass. [*Pause.*] How hot it is! [*Unthinkingly he takes off his coat.*] Oh, sorry! [*He starts putting it on again.*]

ESTELLE: Don't bother. You can stay in your shirt-sleeves. As things are . . .

GARCIN: Just so. [*He drops his coat on the sofa.*] You mustn't be angry with me, Estelle.

ESTELLE: I'm not angry with you.

INEZ: And what about me? Are you angry with me?

ESTELLE: Yes.

[*A short silence.*]

INEZ: Well, Mr Garcin, now you have us in the nude all right. Do you understand things any better for that?

GARCIN: I wonder. Yes, perhaps a trifle better. [*Timidly.*] And now suppose we start trying to help each other?

INEZ: I don't need help.

GARCIN: Inez, they've laid their snare damned cunningly – like a cobweb. If you make any movement, if you raise your hand to fan yourself, Estelle and I feel a little tug. Alone, none of us can save himself or herself; we're linked together inextricably. So you can take your choice. [*A pause.*] Hullo? What's happening?

INEZ: They've let it. The windows are wide open, a man is sitting on my bed. *My* bed, if you please! They've let it, let it! Step in, step in, make yourself at home, you brute! Ah, there's a woman, too. She's going up to him, putting her hands on his shoulders . . . Damn it, why don't they turn the lights on? It's getting dark. Now he's going to kiss her. But that's my room, *my* room! Pitch dark now. I can't see anything, but I hear them whispering, whispering. Is he going to make love to her on *my* bed? What's that she said? That it's noon and the sun is shining? I must be going blind. [*A pause.*] Blacked out. I can't see or hear a thing. So I'm done with the earth, it seems. No more alibis for me! [*She shudders.*] I feel so empty, desiccated – really dead at last. All of me's here, in this room. [*A pause.*] What were you saying? Something about helping me, wasn't it?

GARCIN: Yes.

INEZ: Helping me to do what?

GARCIN: To defeat their devilish tricks.

INEZ: And what do you expect me to do, in return?

GARCIN: To help *me*. It only needs a little effort, Inez; just a spark of human feeling.

INEZ: Human feeling. That's beyond my range. I'm rotten to the core.

GARCIN: And how about me? [*A pause.*] All the same, suppose we try.

INEZ: It's no use. I'm all dried up. I can't give and I can't receive. How could *I* help you? A dead twig, ready for the burning. [*She falls*

silent, gazing at ESTELLE, *who has buried her head in her hands.*]
Florence was fair, a natural blonde.

GARCIN: Do you realize that this young woman's fated to be your torturer?

INEZ: Perhaps I've guessed it.

GARCIN: It's through her they'll get you. I, of course, I'm different . . . . aloof. I take no notice of her. Suppose you had a try . . .

INEZ: Yes?

GARCIN: It's a trap. They're watching you, to see if you'll fall into it.

INEZ: I know. And you're another trap. Do you think they haven't foreknown every word you say? And of course there's a whole nest of pitfalls that we can't see. Everything here's a booby-trap. But what do I care? I'm a pitfall, too. For her, obviously. And perhaps I'll catch her.

GARCIN: You won't catch anything. We're chasing after each other, round and round in a vicious circle, like the horses on a roundabout. That's part of their plan, of course . . . Drop it, Inez. Open your hands and let go of everything. Or else you'll bring disaster on all three of us.

INEZ: Do I look the sort of person who lets go? I know what's coming to me. I'm going to burn, and it's to last for ever. Yes, I *know* everything. But do you think I'll let go? I'll catch her, she'll see you through my eyes, as Florence saw that other man. What's the good of trying to enlist my sympathy? I assure you I know everything, and I can't feel sorry even for myself. A trap! Don't I know it, and that I'm in a trap myself, up to the neck, and there's nothing to be done about it. And, if it suits their book, so much the better!

GARCIN [*gripping her shoulders*]: Well, *I*, anyhow, can feel sorry for you, too. Look at me, we're naked, naked right through and I can see into your heart. That's one link between us. Do you think I'd want to hurt you? I don't regret anything, I'm dried up, too. But for you I can still feel pity.

INEZ [*who has let him keep his hands on her shoulders until now, shakes herself loose*]: Don't. I hate being pawed about. And keep your pity for yourself. Don't forget, Garcin, that there are traps for you, too, in this room. All nicely set for you. You'd do better to watch your own interests. [*A pause.*] But, if you will leave us in peace, this child and me, I'll see I don't do you any harm.

GARCIN [*gazes at her for a moment, then shrugs his shoulders*]: Very well.

ESTELLE [*raising her head*]: Please, Garcin.

GARCIN: What do you want of me?

ESTELLE [*rises and goes up to him*]: You can help *me*, anyhow.

GARCIN: If you want help, apply to her.

[INEZ *has come up and is standing behind* ESTELLE, *but without touching her. During the dialogue that follows she speaks almost in her ear. But* ESTELLE *keeps her eyes on* GARCIN, *who observes her without speaking, and she addresses her answers to him, as if it were he who is questioning her.*]

ESTELLE: I implore you, Garcin . . . you gave me your promise, didn't you? Help me quick. I don't want to be left alone. Olga's taken him to a cabaret.

INEZ: Taken whom?

ESTELLE: Peter . . . Oh, now they're dancing together.

INEZ: Who's Peter?

ESTELLE: Such a silly boy. He called me his glancing stream – just fancy! He was terribly in love with me . . . She's persuaded him to come out with her tonight.

INEZ: Do you love him?

ESTELLE: They're sitting down now. She's puffing like a grampus. What a fool the girl is to insist on dancing! But I dare say she does it to reduce . . . No, of course I don't love him; he's only eighteen, and I'm not a baby-snatcher.

INEZ: Then why bother about them? What difference can it make?

ESTELLE: He belonged to me.

INEZ: Nothing on earth belongs to you any more.

ESTELLE: I tell you he was mine. All mine.

INEZ: Yes, he *was* yours – once. But now – Try to make him hear, try to touch him. Olga can touch him, talk to him as much as she likes. That's so, isn't it? She can squeeze his hands, rub herself against him . . .

ESTELLE: Yes, look! She's pressing her great fat chest against him, puffing and blowing in his face. But, my poor little lamb, can't you see how ridiculous she is, why don't you laugh at her? Oh, once I'd have only had to glance at them, and she'd have slunk away. Is there really nothing, nothing left of me?

INEZ: Nothing whatever. Nothing of you's left on earth – not even

a shadow. All you own is here. Would you like that paper-knife?
Or that ornament on the mantelpiece? That blue sofa's yours. And
I, my dear, am yours for ever.

ESTELLE: You mine! That's good! Well, which of you two would
dare to call me his glancing stream, his crystal girl? You know too
much about me, you know I'm rotten through and through . . .
Peter dear, think of me, fix your thoughts on me, and save me. All
the time you're thinking 'my glancing stream, my crystal girl', I'm
only half here, I'm only half wicked, and half of me is down there
with you, clean and bright and crystal-clear as running water . . .
Oh, just look at her face, all scarlet, like a tomato! No, it's absurd,
we've laughed at her together, you and I, often and often . . .
What's that tune, I always loved it? Yes, the St Louis Blues . . . All
right, dance away, dance away. Garcin, I wish you could see her,
you'd die of laughing. Only – she'll never know I *see* her. Yes, I see
you, Olga, with your hair all anyhow, and you do look a dope, my
dear. Oh, now you're treading on his toes. It's a scream! Hurry up!
Quicker! Quicker! He's dragging her along, bundling her round
and round – it's too ghastly! He always said I was so light, he loved
to dance with me. [*She is dancing as she speaks.*] I tell you, Olga, I
can see you. No, she doesn't care, she's dancing through my gaze.
What's that? What's that you said? 'Our poor dear Estelle'? Oh,
don't be such a humbug! You didn't even shed a tear at the funeral
. . . And she has the nerve to talk to him about her poor dear friend
Estelle! How dare she discuss me with Peter? Now then, keep time.
She never could dance and talk at once. Oh, what's that . . . ? No,
no. Don't tell him. Please, please don't tell him. You can keep him,
do what you like with him, but please don't tell him about – that!
[*She has stopped dancing.*] All right. You can have him now. Isn't it
foul, Garcin? She's told him everything, about Roger, my trip to
Switzerland, the baby. 'Poor Estelle wasn't exactly . . .' No, I wasn't
exactly . . . True enough. He's looking grave, shaking his head, but
he doesn't seem so very much surprised, not what one'd expect.
Keep him then – I won't haggle with you over his long eyelashes,
his pretty girlish face. They're yours for the asking. His glancing
stream, his crystal. Well, the crystal's shattered into bits. 'Poor
Estelle!' Dance, dance, dance. On with it. But do keep time. One,
two. One, two. How I'd love to go down to earth for just a

moment, and dance with him again. [*She dances again for some moments.*] The music's growing fainter. They've turned down the lights, like they do for a tango. Why are they playing so softly? Louder, please. I can't hear. It's so far away, so far away. I . . . I can't hear a sound. [*She stops dancing.*] All over. It's the end. The earth has left me. [*To* GARCIN.] Don't turn from me . . . please. Take me in your arms.

[*Behind* ESTELLE'S *back,* INEZ *signs to* GARCIN *to move away.*]

INEZ [*commandingly*]: Now then, Garcin!

[GARCIN *moves back a step, and, glancing at* ESTELLE, *points to* INEZ.]

GARCIN: It's to her you should say that.

ESTELLE [*clinging to him*]: Don't turn away. You're a man, aren't you, and surely I'm not such a fright as all that! Everyone says I've lovely hair and, after all, a man killed himself on my account. You have to look at something, and there's nothing here to see except the sofas and that awful ornament and the table. Surely I'm better to look at than a lot of stupid furniture. Listen! I've dropped out of their hearts like a little sparrow fallen from its nest. So gather me up, dear, fold me to your heart – and you'll see how nice I can be.

GARCIN [*freeing himself from her, after a short struggle*]: I tell you it's to that lady you should speak.

ESTELLE: To her? But she doesn't count, she's a woman.

INEZ: Oh, I don't count? Is that what you think? But, my poor little fallen nestling, you've been sheltering in my heart for ages, though you didn't realize it. Don't be afraid; I'll keep looking at you for ever and ever, without a flutter of my eyelids, and you'll live in my gaze like a mote in a sunbeam.

ESTELLE: A sunbeam indeed! Don't talk such rubbish! You've tried that trick already, and you should know it doesn't work.

INEZ: Estelle! My glancing stream! My crystal!

ESTELLE: *Your* crystal? It's grotesque. Do you think you can fool me with that sort of talk? Everyone knows by now what I did to my baby. The crystal's shattered, but I don't care. I'm just a hollow dummy, all that's left of me is the outside – but it's not for you.

INEZ: Come to me, Estelle. You shall be whatever you like: a glancing stream, a muddy stream. And deep down in my eyes you'll see yourself just as you want to be.

ESTELLE: Oh, leave me in peace. You haven't any eyes. Oh, damn it, isn't there anything I can do to get rid of you? I've an idea. [*She spits in* INEZ' *face.*] There!

INEZ: Garcin, you shall pay for this.

[*A pause.* GARCIN *shrugs his shoulders and goes to* ESTELLE.]

GARCIN: So it's a man you need?

ESTELLE: Not *any* man. You.

GARCIN: No humbug now. Any man would do your business. As I happen to be here, you want me. Right! [*He grips her shoulders.*] Mind, I'm not your sort at all, really, I'm not a young nincompoop and I don't dance the tango.

ESTELLE: I'll take you as you are. And perhaps I shall change you.

GARCIN: I doubt it. I shan't pay much attention: I've other things to think about.

ESTELLE: What things?

GARCIN: They wouldn't interest you.

ESTELLE: I'll sit on your sofa and wait for you to take some notice of me. I promise not to bother you at all.

INEZ [*with a shrill laugh*]: That's right, fawn on him, like the silly bitch you are. Grovel and cringe! And he hasn't even good looks to commend him!

ESTELLE [*to* GARCIN]: Don't listen to her. She has no eyes, no ears. She's – nothing.

GARCIN: I'll give you what I can. It doesn't amount to much. I shan't love you; I know you too well.

ESTELLE: Do you want me, anyhow?

GARCIN: Yes.

ESTELLE: I ask no more.

GARCIN: In that case . . . [*He bends over her.*]

INEZ: Estelle! Garcin! You must be going crazy. You're not alone. I'm here too.

GARCIN: Of course – but what does it matter?

INEZ: Under my eyes? You couldn't . . . couldn't do it.

ESTELLE: Why not? I often undressed with my maid looking on.

INEZ [*gripping* GARCIN'S *arm*]: Let her alone. Don't paw her with your dirty man's hands.

GARCIN [*thrusting her away roughly*]: Take care. I'm no gentleman and I'd have no compunction about striking a woman.

INEZ: But you promised me; you promised. I'm only asking you to keep your word.

GARCIN: Why should I, considering you were the first to break our agreement?

[INEZ *turns her back on him and retreats to the far end of the room.*]

INEZ: Very well, have it your own way. I'm the weaker party, one against two. But don't forget I'm here, and watching. I shan't take my eyes off you, Garcin; when you're kissing her, you'll feel them boring into you. Yes, have it your own way, make love and get it over. We're in hell; my turn will come.

[*During the following scene she watches them without speaking.*]

GARCIN [*coming back to* ESTELLE *and grasping her shoulders*]: Now then. Your lips. Give me your lips.

[*A pause. He bends to kiss her; then abruptly straightens up.*]

ESTELLE [*indignantly*]: Really! [*A pause.*] Didn't I tell you not to pay any attention to her?

GARCIN: You've got it wrong. [*Short silence.*] It's Gomez; he's back in the press-room. They've shut the windows; it must be winter down there. Six months. Six months since I . . . Well, I warned you I'd be absent-minded sometimes, didn't I? They're shivering, they've kept their coats on. Funny they should feel the cold like that, when I'm feeling so hot. Ah, this time he's talking about me.

ESTELLE: Is it going to last long? [*Short silence.*] You might at least tell me what he's saying.

GARCIN: Nothing. Nothing worth repeating. He's a swine, that's all. [*He listens attentively.*] A god-damned, bloody swine. [*He turns to* ESTELLE.] Let's come back to – to ourselves. Are you going to love me?

ESTELLE [*smiling*]: I wonder now!

GARCIN: Will you trust me?

ESTELLE: What a quaint thing to ask! Considering you'll be under my eyes all the time, and I don't think I've much to fear from Inez, so far as you're concerned.

GARCIN: Obviously. [*A pause. He takes his hands off* ESTELLE'S *shoulders.*] I was thinking of another kind of trust. [*Listens.*] Talk away, talk away, you swine. I'm not there to defend myself. [*To* ESTELLE.] Estelle, you *must* give me your trust.

ESTELLE: Oh, what a nuisance you are! I'm giving you my mouth

my arms, my whole body – and everything could be so simple . . .
My trust! I haven't any to give, I'm afraid, and you're making me
terribly embarrassed. You must have something pretty ghastly on
your conscience to make such a fuss about my trusting you.

GARCIN: They shot me.

ESTELLE: I know. Because you refused to fight. Well, why shouldn't
you?

GARCIN: I . . . I didn't exactly refuse. [*In a far-away voice.*] I must say
he talks well, he makes out a good case against me, but he never
says what I should have done, instead. Should I have gone to the
General and said, 'General, I decline to fight'? A mug's game; they'd
have promptly locked me up. But I wanted to show my colours,
my true colours, do you understand? I wasn't going to be silenced.
[*To* ESTELLE.] So I . . . I took the train . . . They caught me at the
frontier.

ESTELLE: Where were you trying to go?

GARCIN: To Mexico. I meant to launch a pacifist newspaper down
there. [*A short silence.*] Well, why don't you speak?

ESTELLE: What could I say? You acted quite rightly, as you didn't
want to fight. [GARCIN *makes a fretful gesture.*] But, darling, how on
earth can I guess what you want me to answer?

INEZ: Can't you guess? Well, *I* can. He wants you to tell him that
he bolted like a lion. For 'bolt' he did, and that's what's biting
him.

GARCIN: 'Bolted', 'went away' – we won't quarrel over words.

ESTELLE: But you *had* to run away. If you'd stayed they'd have sent
you to jail, wouldn't they?

GARCIN: Of course. [*A pause.*] Well, Estelle, am I a coward?

ESTELLE: How can I say? Don't be so unreasonable, darling. I can't
put myself in your skin. You must decide that for yourself.

GARCIN [*wearily*]: I can't decide.

ESTELLE: Anyhow, you must remember. You must have had reasons
for acting as you did.

GARCIN: I had.

ESTELLE: Well?

GARCIN: But were they the real reasons?

ESTELLE: You've a twisted mind, that's your trouble. Plaguing yourself over such trifles!

GARCIN: I'd thought it all out, and I wanted to make a stand. But was that my real motive?

INEZ: Exactly. That's the question. Was that your real motive? No doubt you argued it out with yourself, you weighed the pros and cons, you found good reasons for acting as you did. But fear and hatred and all the dirty little instincts one keeps dark – they're motives too. So carry on, Mr Garcin, and try to be honest with yourself – for once.

GARCIN: Do I need you to tell me that? Day and night I paced my cell, from the window to the door, from the door to the window. I pried into my heart, I sleuthed myself like a detective. By the end of it I felt as if I'd given my whole life to introspection. But always I harked back to the one thing certain – that I had acted as I did, I'd taken that train to the frontier. But why? Why? Finally I thought: My death will settle it. If I face death courageously, I'll prove I am no coward.

INEZ: And how did you face death?

GARCIN: Miserably. Rottenly. [INEZ laughs.] Oh, it was only a physical lapse – that might happen to anyone; I'm not ashamed of it. Only everything's been left in suspense, for ever. [To ESTELLE.] Come here, Estelle. Look at me. I want to feel someone looking at me while they're talking about me on earth . . . I like green eyes.

INEZ: Green eyes! Just hark to him! And you, Estelle, do you like cowards?

ESTELLE: If you knew how little I care! Coward or hero, it's all one – provided he kisses well.

GARCIN: There they are, slumped in their chairs, sucking at their cigars. Bored they look. Half-asleep. They're thinking: Garcin's a coward. But only vaguely, dreamily. One's got to think of something. 'That chap Garcin was a coward.' That's what they've decided, those dear friends of mine. In six months' time they'll be saying, 'Cowardly as that skunk Garcin'. You're lucky, you two; no one on earth is giving you another thought. But I – I'm long in dying.

INEZ: What about your wife, Garcin?

GARCIN: Oh, didn't I tell you? She's dead.

INEZ: Dead?

GARCIN: Yes, she died just now. About two months ago.

INEZ: Of grief?

GARCIN: What else should she die of? So all is for the best, you see;
the war's over, my wife's dead, and I've carved out my place in
history.

[*He gives a choking sob and passes his hand over his face.* ESTELLE
catches his arm.]

ESTELLE: My poor darling! Look at me. Please look. Touch me.
Touch me. [*She takes his hand and puts it on her neck.*] There! Keep
your hand there. [GARCIN *makes a fretful movement.*] No, don't
move. Why trouble what those men are thinking? They'll die off
one by one. Forget them. There's only me, now.

GARCIN: But *they* won't forget *me*, not they! They'll die, but others
will come after them to carry on the legend. I've left my fate in
their hands.

ESTELLE: You think too much, that's your trouble.

GARCIN: What else is there to do now? I was a man of action once . . .
Oh, if only I could be with them again, for just one day – I'd fling
their lie in their teeth. But I'm locked out; they're passing judge-
ment on my life without troubling about me, and they're right,
because I'm dead. Dead and done with. [*Laughs.*] A back number.

[*A short pause.*]

ESTELLE [*gently*]: Garcin.

GARCIN: Still there? Now listen! I want you to do me a service. No,
don't shrink away. I know it must seem strange to you, having
someone asking you for help; you're not used to that. But if you'll
make the effort, if you'll only *will* it hard enough, I dare say we can
really love each other. Look at it this way. A thousand of them are
proclaiming I'm a coward; but what do numbers matter? If there's
someone, just one person, to say quite positively I did not run away,
that I'm not the sort who runs away, that I'm brave and decent and
the rest of it – well, that one person's faith would save me. Will you
have that faith in me? Then I shall love you and cherish you for
ever. Estelle – will you?

ESTELLE [*laughing*]: Oh, you dear silly man, do you think I could love
a coward?

GARCIN: But just now you said –

ESTELLE: I was only teasing you. I like men, my dear, who're real
men, with tough skin and strong hands. You haven't a coward's

chin, or a coward's mouth, or a coward's voice, or a coward's hair. And it's for your mouth, your hair, your voice, I love you.

GARCIN: Do you mean this? *Really* mean it?

ESTELLE: Shall I swear it?

GARCIN: Then I snap my fingers at them all, those below and those in here. Estelle, we shall climb out of hell. [INEZ *gives a shrill laugh. He breaks off and stares at her.*] What's that?

INEZ [*still laughing*]: But she doesn't mean a word of what she says. How can you be such a simpleton? 'Estelle, am I a coward?' As if she cared a damn either way.

ESTELLE: Inez, how dare you? [*To* GARCIN.] Don't listen to her. If you want me to have faith in you, you must begin by trusting me.

INEZ: That's right! That's right! Trust away! She wants a man – that far you can trust her – she wants a man's arm round her waist, a man's smell, a man's eyes glowing with desire. And that's all she wants. She'd assure you you were God Almighty if she thought it would give you pleasure.

GARCIN: Estelle, is this true? Answer me. Is it true?

ESTELLE: What do you expect me to say? Don't you realize how maddening it is to have to answer questions one can't make head or tail of? [*She stamps her foot.*] You do make things difficult . . . Anyhow, I'd love you just the same, even if you were a coward. Isn't that enough?

[*A short pause.*]

GARCIN [*to the two women*]: You disgust me, both of you. [*He goes towards the door.*]

ESTELLE: What are you up to?

GARCIN: I'm going.

INEZ [*quickly*]: You won't get far. The door is locked.

GARCIN: I'll *make* them open it. [*He presses the bell-push. The bell does not ring.*]

ESTELLE: Please! Please!

INEZ [*to* ESTELLE]: Don't worry, my pet. The bell doesn't work.

GARCIN: I tell you they shall open. [*Drums on the door.*] I can't endure it any longer, I'm through with you both. [ESTELLE *runs to him; he pushes her away.*] Go away. You're even fouler than she. I won't let myself get bogged in your eyes. You're soft and slimy. Ugh! [*Bangs on the door again.*] Like an octopus. Like a quagmire.

ESTELLE: I beg you, oh I beg you not to leave me. I'll promise not to speak again, I won't trouble you in any way – but don't go. I daren't be left alone with Inez, now she's shown her claws.

GARCIN: Look after yourself. I never asked you to come here.

ESTELLE: Oh, how mean you are! Yes, it's quite true you're a coward.

INEZ [*going up to* ESTELLE]: Well, my little sparrow fallen from the nest, I hope you're satisfied now. You spat in my face – playing up to him, of course – and we had a tiff on his account. But he's going, and a good riddance it will be. We two women will have the place to ourselves.

ESTELLE: You won't gain anything. If that door opens, I'm going, too.

INEZ: Where?

ESTELLE: I don't care where. As far from you as I can.

[GARCIN *has been drumming on the door while they talk.*]

GARCIN: Open the door! Open, blast you! I'll endure anything, your red-hot tongs and molten lead, your racks and prongs and garrottes – all your fiendish gadgets, everything that burns and flays and tears – I'll put up with any torture you impose. Anything, anything would be better than this agony of mind, this creeping pain that gnaws and fumbles and caresses one, and never hurts quite enough. [*He grips the door-knob and rattles it.*] Now will you open? [*The door flies open with a jerk, and he nearly falls on the floor.*] Ah! [*A long silence.*]

INEZ: Well, Garcin? . . . You're free to go.

GARCIN [*meditatively*]: Now I wonder why that door opened.

INEZ: What are you waiting for? Hurry up and go.

GARCIN: I shall not go.

INEZ: And you, Estelle? [ESTELLE *does not move.* INEZ *bursts out laughing.*] So what? Which shall it be? Which of the three of us will leave? The barrier's down, why are we waiting? . . . But what a situation! It's a scream! We're . . . inseparables!

[ESTELLE *springs at her from behind.*]

ESTELLE: Inseparables? Garcin, come and lend a hand. Quickly. We'll push her out and slam the door on her. That'll teach her a lesson.

INEZ [*struggling with* ESTELLE]: Estelle! I beg you, let me stay. I won't go, I won't go! Not into the passage.

GARCIN: Let go of her.

ESTELLE: You're crazy. She hates you.

GARCIN: It's because of her I'm staying here.

[ESTELLE *releases* INEZ *and stares dumbfoundedly at* GARCIN.]

INEZ: Because of me? [*Pause.*] All right, shut the door. It's ten times hotter here since it opened. [GARCIN *goes to the door and shuts it.*] Because of me, you said?

GARCIN: Yes. *You*, anyhow, know what it means to be a coward.

INEZ: Yes, I know.

GARCIN: And you know what wickedness is, and shame, and fear. There were days when you peered into yourself, into the secret places of your heart, and what you saw there made you faint with horror. And then, next day, you didn't know what to make of it, you couldn't interpret the horror you had glimpsed the day before. Yes, you know what evil *costs*. And when you say I'm a coward, you know from experience what that means. Is that so?

INEZ: Yes.

GARCIN: So it's you whom I have to convince; you are of my kind. Did you suppose I meant to go? No, I couldn't leave you here, gloating over my defeat, with all those thoughts about me running in your head.

INEZ: Do you really wish to convince me?

GARCIN: That's the one and only thing I wish for now. I can't hear them any longer, you know. Probably that means they're through with me. For good and all. The curtain's down, nothing of me is left on earth – not even the name of coward. So, Inez, we're alone. Only you two remain to give a thought to me. She – she doesn't count. It's you who matter; you who hate me. If you'll have faith in me I'm saved.

INEZ: It won't be easy. Have a look at me. I'm a hard-headed woman.

GARCIN: I'll give you all the time that's needed.

INEZ: Yes, we've lots of time in hand. *All* time.

GARCIN [*putting his hands on her shoulders*]: Listen! Each man has an aim in life, a leading motive; that's so, isn't it? Well, I didn't give a damn for wealth, or for love. I aimed at being a real man. A tough, as they say. I staked everything on the same horse . . . Can one possibly be a coward when one's deliberately courted danger at every turn? And can one judge a life by a single action?

INEZ: Why not? For thirty years you dreamt you were a hero, and condoned a thousand petty lapses – because a hero, of course, can do no wrong. An easy method, obviously. Then a day came when you were up against it, the red light of real danger – and you took the train to Mexico.

GARCIN: I 'dreamt', you say. It was no dream. When I chose the hardest path, I made my choice deliberately. A man is what he wills himself to be.

INEZ: Prove it. Prove it was no dream. It's what one does, and nothing else, that shows the stuff one's made of.

GARCIN: I died too soon. I wasn't allowed time to . . . to do my deeds.

INEZ: One always dies too soon – or too late. And yet one's whole life is complete at that moment, with a line drawn neatly under it, ready for the summing up. You are – your life, and nothing else.

GARCIN: What a poisonous woman you are! With an answer for everything.

INEZ: Now then! Don't lose heart. It shouldn't be so hard, convincing me. Pull yourself together, man, rake up some arguments. [GARCIN *shrugs his shoulders.*] Ah, wasn't I right when I said you were vulnerable? Now you're going to pay the price, and what a price! You're a coward, Garcin, because I wish it. I wish it – do you hear? – I wish it. And yet, just look at me, see how weak I am, a mere breath on the air, a gaze observing you, a formless thought that thinks you. [*He walks towards her, opening his hands.*] Ah, they're open now, those big hands, those coarse, man's hands! But what do you hope to do? You can't throttle thoughts with hands. So you've no choice, you must convince me, and you're at my mercy.

ESTELLE: Garcin!

GARCIN: What?

ESTELLE: Revenge yourself.

GARCIN: How?

ESTELLE: Kiss me, darling – then you'll hear her squeal.

GARCIN: That's true, Inez. I'm at your mercy, but you're at mine as well.

[*He bends over* ESTELLE. INEZ *gives a little cry.*]

INEZ: Oh, you coward, you weakling, running to women to console you!

ESTELLE: That's right, Inez. Squeal away.

INEZ: What a lovely pair you make! If you could see his big paw splayed out on your back, rucking up your skin and creasing the silk. Be careful, though! He's perspiring, his hand will leave a blue stain on your dress.

ESTELLE: Squeal away, Inez, squeal away! . . . Hug me tight, darling; tighter still – that'll finish her off, and a good thing too!

INEZ: Yes, Garcin, she's right. Carry on with it, press her to you till you feel your bodies melting into each other; a lump of warm, throbbing flesh . . . Love's a grand solace, isn't it, my friend? Deep and dark as sleep. But I'll see you don't sleep.

[GARCIN *makes a slight movement.*]

ESTELLE: Don't listen to her. Press your lips to my mouth. Oh, I'm yours, yours, yours.

INEZ: Well, what are you waiting for? Do as you're told. What a lovely scene: coward Garcin holding baby-killer Estelle in his manly arms! Make your stakes, everyone. Will coward Garcin kiss the lady, or won't he dare? What's the betting? I'm watching you, everybody's watching, I'm a crowd all by myself. Do you hear the crowd? Do you hear them muttering, Garcin? Mumbling and muttering. 'Coward! Coward! Coward! Coward!' – that's what they're saying . . . It's no use trying to escape, I'll never let you go. What do you hope to get from her silly lips? Forgetfulness? But I shan't forget you, not I! 'It's I you must convince.' So come to me, I'm waiting. Come alone now . . . Look how obedient he is, like a well-trained dog who comes when his mistress calls. You can't hold him, and you never will.

GARCIN: Will night never come?

INEZ: Never.

GARCIN: You will always see me?

INEZ: Always.

[GARCIN *moves away from* ESTELLE *and takes some steps across the room. He goes to the bronze ornament.*]

GARCIN: This bronze. [*Strokes it thoughtfully.*] Yes, now's the moment; I'm looking at this thing on the mantelpiece, and I understand that I'm in hell. I tell you, everything's been thought out beforehand. They knew I'd stand at the fireplace stroking this thing of bronze, with all those eyes intent on me. Devouring me. [*He swings round abruptly.*] What? Only two of you? I thought there were more; many more. [*Laughs.*] So this is hell. I'd never have believed it. You remember all we were told about the torture-chambers, the fire and brimstone, the 'burning marl'. Old wives' tales! There's no need for red-hot pokers. Hell is . . . other people!

ESTELLE: My darling! Please . . .

GARCIN [*thrusting her away*]: No, let me be. She is between us. I cannot love you when she's watching.

ESTELLE: Right! In that case, I'll stop her watching us.

[*She picks up the paper-knife from the table, rushes at* INEZ, *and stabs her several times.*]

INEZ [*struggling and laughing*]: But, you crazy creature, what do you think you're doing? You know quite well I'm dead.

ESTELLE: Dead?

[*She drops the knife. A pause.* INEZ *picks up the knife and jabs herself with it regretfully.*]

INEZ: Dead! Dead! Dead! Knives, poison, ropes – all useless. It has happened *already*, do you understand? Once and for all. So here we are, for ever. [*Laughs.*]

ESTELLE [*with a peal of laughter*]: For ever. My God, how funny! For ever.

GARCIN [*looks at the two women, and joins in the laughter*]: For ever, and ever, and ever.

[*They slump on to their respective sofas. A long silence. Their laughter dies away, and they gaze at each other.*]

GARCIN: Well, well, let's get on with it . . .

CURTAIN